GULISTAN ILLUSTRATED

THE ROSE GARDEN

GULISTAN ILLUSTRATED
THE ROSE GARDEN

13TH CENTURY PERSIAN POEMS AND STORIES

SA'DI SHĪRĀZĪ

Amber Books Ltd
United House
North Road
London N7 9DP
United Kingdom
www.amberbooks.co.uk
Facebook: amberbooks
YouTube: amberbooksltd
Instagram: amberbooksltd
X(Twitter): @amberbooks

ISBN: 978-1-83886-592-4

Editorial, Design and Picture Research: Amber Books Ltd

Consultant Editor:
Dr. Mahdi Salari Nasab holds degrees in Philosophy and Public Law from the University of Tehran and Shahid Beheshti University in Iran. He has published various titles in Persian literature, including *Rumi Illustrated, An Introduction to Masnavi Ma'navi of Rumi, The Book of Shams-e Tabrizi* and *Living in Words: examining the intellectual and artistic heritage of Rumi.*

Printed and bound in China

TRADITIONAL CHINESE BOOKBINDING
This book has been produced using traditional Chinese bookbinding techniques, using a method that was developed during the Ming Dynasty (1368–1644) and remained in use until the adoption of Western binding techniques in the early 1900s. In traditional Chinese binding, single sheets of paper are printed on one side only, and each sheet is folded in half, with the printed pages on the outside. The book block is then sandwiched between two boards and sewn together through punched holes close to the cut edges of the folded sheets.

CONTENTS

EDITOR'S INTRODUCTION

This edition presents a selection from Sa'di's *Gulistan*[1], based on the English translation by Edward Rehatsek. Below are some key points regarding this edition:

1. We have tried to ensure that this selection captures the literary, intellectual, educational and moral dimensions of Sa'di's *Gulistan.*

2. Our aim has been to showcase significant narratives and themes from the entire text of *Gulistan*, encompassing both the introduction and the eight chapters.

3. More than half of *Gulistan* is included in this selection.

4. To enhance clarity, especially for non-Persian speakers, we have omitted content that may be less relevant today, such as passages containing religious biases or praise of kings, as well as material that requires specific knowledge of Persian vocabulary nuances.

5. A distinguishing feature of this edition, compared with all previously published versions – whether complete or abridged – is the use of different fonts to separate and highlight various elements of the original work. This allows readers to easily identify the main prose sections from the poetry (italicized verse), proverbs and aphorisms (in small capitals), and quotes from the Quran (italicized small capitals).

6. It is noteworthy that Iranian culture is rich in proverbs and wisdom literature. Within this context, *Gulistan* contains an abundance of proverbs, which serve as distilled expressions of Iranian wisdom. By distinguishing these proverbs within Sa'di's prose and poetry, readers gain insight into some of the wisdom of this culture.

[1] In some sources, it is also written with this English spelling: *Golestan.*

About Sa'di and Gulistan[3]

Sa'di – Abu Mohammad Mošarref-al-Din Mosleh b. 'Abd-Allāh b. Mošarref Širāzi, Persian poet and prose writer (b. Shiraz, 1210; d. Shiraz, 1291 or 1292) – is widely recognized as one of the greatest masters of the classical literary tradition.

When Sa'di returned to Shiraz around 1257 after some 30 years of travel, he was apparently already a famous and highly respected poet, a fame that must have been based on the wide circulation of his masterful ghazals.

The two most reliable dates in Sa'di's biography are the dates of the completion of his two best-known books, the *Bustan* and the *Gulistan*. The *Bustan* was completed late in the year of 1257, after Sa'di's return to Shiraz following his extended absence. The *Gulistan* was completed a year later in 1258.

Although Sa'di spent the final decades of his life in Shiraz, his poetry and reputation spread throughout the Persophone world, travelling even to places that he probably never visited in person.

Sa'di lived through one of the most eventful and traumatic centuries in the history of Asia and the Middle East. The expansion and consolidation of Mongol power was marked by the destruction of old centres of culture and civilization, the upheaval of established political institutions and the mass migration of populations. Sa'di met the challenges of his age by adept and constant motion. In his early years, this motion was physical; as an itinerant scholar and increasingly respected poet, his mastery of language and literate culture allowed him to move from place to place and in and out of mosques, markets and palaces. He maintained a social mobility even after settling in Shiraz. His works show that he was in regular contact with the ruling circles of the city.

The irony, humour and charity of judgement that are often found in his writings result from an ability to maintain multiple perspectives and an

[3] Derived from *The Encyclopaedia Iranica*, entries on 'Sa'di' and the 'Golestan of Sa'di', by Paul Losensky and Franklin Lewis, with summarization and slight modifications.

7. In existing editions of *Gulistan*, verses that follow one another but belong to different poems are often printed without spacing, making it difficult for non-Persian speakers, even for non-specialist Persian speakers, to discern this distinction. In this edition, verses from different poems that appear consecutively are separated by spaces and bullet points, clearly indicating their distinctiveness.

8. This edition has been prepared with accuracy and completeness, aligning with Edward Rehatsek's original translation and the most authoritative editions of *Gulistan* in Tehran[2], correcting several errors found in Rehatsek's work.

9. Thus, by engaging with this selection, readers can claim access to the essence of Sa'di's *Gulistan* – one of the most important works in Persian and world literature – made available in English based on the most credible Persian editions.

10. Following this introduction, readers will find a brief overview of Sa'di's life and *Gulistan*. This will be succeeded by Edward Rehatsek's preface to the original work, followed by the main text.

Mahdi Salarinasab
January 2025

[2] The two most authoritative edits of Sa'di's *Gulistan* were done by Mohammad-Ali Foroughi and Gholam-Hossein Yousofi.

awareness of his own fallibility. This detachment is nevertheless informed by a commitment to certain core values: concern for the suffering of others (especially the less privileged), awareness of the fragility of life, and faith in a moral reckoning, both in this life and the next. Sa'di's concern for social welfare requires an engagement with the politically powerful, but also a circumspect caution and a willingness to adapt principle to the particular situation at hand. Similarly, the works acknowledge the need for religious authority, but also recognize the hypocrisy and self-righteousness that often accompany it. Despite the dire times through which the author lived, Sa'di's works project a joy and vitality that seems to grow from his full participation in two capacities that most make us human: love and language. His works celebrate love in its manifold forms – social solidarity, friendship, amorous desire and religious devotion – and they do so in a language that revels in the full capacities of the linguistic medium to range from dignified balance and aphoristic concision to playful punning and raucous excess.

His collected works in verse and prose are known by the generic title of *Kolliāt* ('Collected Works').

The most important works of Sa'di include:
Poems:

1. *Bustān*
2. Ghazals
3. Persian *qasidas*
4. Arabic *qasidas*
5. Fragments
6. Quatrains.

Prose:

1. *Gulistān* (mixed with poetry)
2. Five sermons
3. Treatise on reason and love
4. Advice to kings
5. Jokes and humorous diversions.

The *Gulistan of Sa'di*, probably the single most influential work of prose in the Persian tradition, was completed in 1258.

Sa'di describes the *Gulistan* as primarily entertaining, but explains his purpose as delivering sermons and counsel in a palatable form. He does this with deliberate terseness and concision through anecdotes and witticisms, parables, tales and reports about the conduct of the kings of the past. Sa'di narrates these in prose, typically reserving verse to punctuate the narrative with commentary or draw a moral from it. The narratives range in length from jokes delivered in a short sentence or two, to stories which unfold over several pages.

Tadhib *(Shamseh), unknown artist, Indo Iranian Album.*

INTRODUCTORY

Laudation to the God of majesty and glory! Obedience to him is a cause of approach and gratitude in increase of benefits.

EVERY INHALATION OF THE BREATH PROLONGS LIFE AND EVERY EXPIRATION OF IT GLADDENS OUR NATURE; WHEREFORE EVERY BREATH CONFERS TWO BENEFITS AND FOR EVERY BENEFIT GRATITUDE IS DUE.

Whose hand and tongue is capable
To fulfil the obligations of thanks to him?

The showers of his boundless mercy have penetrated to every spot, and the banquet of his unstinted liberality is spread out everywhere. He tears not the veil of reputation of his worshippers even for grievous sins, and does not withhold their daily allowance of bread for great crimes.

He told the chamberlain of the morning breeze to spread out the emerald carpet and, having commanded the nurse of vernal clouds to cherish the daughters of plants in the cradle of the earth, the trees donned the new year's robe and clothed their breast with the garment of green foliage, whilst their offspring, the branches, adorned their heads with blossoms at the approach of the season of the roses. Also, the juice of the cane became delicious honey by his power, and the date a lofty tree by his care.

Cloud and wind, moon and sun move in the sky
That thou mayest gain bread, and not eat it unconcerned.
For thee all are revolving and obedient.
It is against the requirements of justice if thou obeyest not.

Those who attend permanently at the temple of his glory confess the imperfection of their worship and say: 'We have not worshipped thee according to the requirements of thy worship'; and those who describe the splendour of his beauty are rapt in amazement saying: 'We have not known thee as thou oughtest to be known.'

Translator's Preface

To produce this new translation of the *Gulistan* of Sheikh Sa'di Shirazi may appear presumptuous and superfluous after the publication of so many others. There is, however, one reason which may justify it in the opinion of persons who do not care in works of this class so much for elegance as for fidelity; and indeed how could the spirit, the mode of thinking, and the style of writing of a work composed in a preceding age, say about six centuries ago, become really known, if it is reproduced in the present, chiefly with a view to suit modern ideas of propriety, carefully disregarding anything which might shock them, and consequently giving only imperfect renderings of such portions as happen to be repugnant to them? It is generally believed that the translations of the *Gulistan* which have hitherto appeared are such expurgated ones, and therefore likewise in that respect deficient in fidelity. How far this is the case anyone may ascertain who will take the trouble to compare other renderings with the present translation, which is as literal as compatible with the English language, and contains the whole work without any attempts at elegance, glossing over, or omitting, whole passages or single expressions not suitable for family reading. As to the original Persian work, there is but little difference between the older honest editions of it which contain the full text; there must, however, be discrepancies in translations whose chief aim is not fidelity, and the translator has purposely avoided consulting any of them, for fear of being tempted to imitate elegant language to the detriment of fidelity.

Edward Rehatsek[4]
(Preface to the original edition, 1888)

[4] Edward Rehatsek (born in 1819 in the town of Ilok – previously in Hungary and now in Croatia – died in Bombay on 11 December 1891) was an Orientalist and translator of several works of Iranian and Islamic literature including the *Golestan* of Sa'di Shirazi.

If someone asks me for his description,
What shall I despairing say of One who has no form?
The lovers have been slain by the beloved.
No voice can come from the slain.

One of the devout who had deeply plunged his head into the cowl of meditation and had been immersed in the ocean of visions, was asked, when he had come out of that state, by one of his companions: 'What beautiful gift hast thou brought us from the garden in which thou hast been?' He replied: 'I intended to fill the skirts of my robe with roses, when I reached the rose-tree, as presents for my friends but the perfume of the flowers intoxicated me so much that I let go the hold of my skirts.'

O bird of the morning, learn love from the moth
Because it burnt, lost its life, and found no voice.
These pretenders are ignorantly in search of Him,
Because he who obtained knowledge has not returned.

•

O thou who art above all imaginations, conjectures, opinions and ideas,
Above anything people have said or we have heard or read,
The assembly is finished and life has reached its term
And we have, as at first, remained powerless in describing thee.

Page from Moraqqa'-e Golshan.

The Cause for Composing the Gulistan

I was one night meditating on the time which had elapsed, repenting of the life I had squandered and perforating the stony mansion of my heart with adamantine tears. I uttered the following verses in conformity with the state of mind:

Every moment a breath of life is spent,
If I consider, not much of it remains.
O thou, whose fifty years have elapsed in sleep,
Wilt thou perhaps overtake them in these five days?
Shame on him who has gone and done no work.
The drum of departure was beaten but he has not made his load.
Sweet sleep on the morning of departure
Retains the pedestrian from the road.
Whoever had come had built a new edifice.
He departed and left the place to another
And that other one concocted the same futile schemes
And this edifice was not completed by anyone.
Cherish not an inconstant friend.
Such a traitor is not fit for amity.
As all the good and bad must surely die,
He is happy who carries off the ball of virtue.
Send provision for thy journey to thy tomb.
Nobody will bring it after thee; send it before.
Life is snow, the sun is melting hot.
Little remains, but the gentleman is slothful still.
O thou who hast gone empty handed to the bazar,
I fear thou wilt not bring a towel filled.
Who eats the corn he has sown while it is yet green,
Must at harvest time glean the ears of it.

After maturely considering these sentiments, I thought proper to sit down in the mansion of retirement to fold up the skirts of association, to wash my tablets of heedless sayings and no more to indulge in senseless prattle:

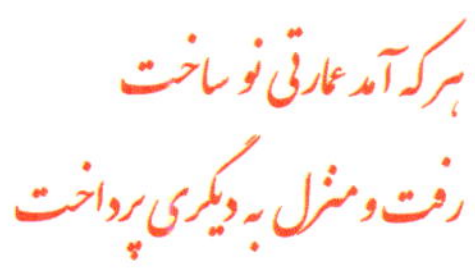

To sit in a corner, like one with a cut tongue, deaf and dumb,
Is better than a man who has no command over his tongue.

I continued in this resolution till a friend, who had been my companion and my comrade in the closet of affection, entered at the door, according to his old custom with playful gladness, and spread out the surface of desire; but I would give him no reply nor lift up my head from the knees of worship. He looked at me aggrieved and said:

'Now, while thou hast the power of utterance,
Speak, O brother, with grace and kindness
Because tomorrow, when the messenger of death arrives,
Thou wilt of necessity restrain thy tongue.'

One of my connections informed him how matters stood and told him that I had firmly determined and was intent upon spending the rest of my life in continual devotion and silence, advising him at the same time, in case he should be able, to follow my example and to keep me company. He replied: 'I swear by the great dignity of Allah and by our old friendship that I shall not draw breath, nor budge one step, unless he converses with me as formerly, and in his usual way, because it is foolish to insult friends and easy to expiate an oath. It is against propriety, and contrary to the opinions of wise men that the Zulfiqar of A'li should remain in the scabbard and the tongue of Sa'di in his palate.

O intelligent man what is the tongue in the mouth?
It is the key to the treasure-door of a virtuous man.
When the door is closed how can one know
Whether he is a seller of jewels or a hawker?

•

Although intelligent men consider silence civil,
It is better for thee to speak at the proper time.

Two things betoken levity of intellect: to remain mute
When it is proper to speak and to talk when silence is required.

In short, I had not the firmness to restrain my tongue from speaking to him, and did not consider it polite to turn away my face from his conversation, he being a congenial friend and sincerely affectionate.

When thou fightest with anyone, consider
Whether thou wilt have to flee from him or he from thee.

I was under the necessity of speaking and then went out by way of diversion in the vernal season, when the traces of severe cold had disappeared and the time of the dominion of roses had arrived:

Green garments were upon the trees
Like holiday robes on contented persons.
On the first of the month Ordibehesht -e Jalali[5]
The bulbuls were singing on the pulpits of branches.
Upon the roses pearls of dew had fallen,
Resembling perspiration on an angry sweetheart's cheek.

I happened to spend the night in a garden with one of my friends and we found it to be a pleasant cheerful place with heart-ravishing entangled trees; its ground seemed to be paved with small glass beads whilst, from its vines, bunches like the Pleiads were suspended.

A garden the water of whose river was limpid
A grove the melody of whose birds was harmonious.
The former full of bright-coloured tulips,
The latter full of fruits of various kinds;
The wind had in the shade of its trees
Spread out a bed of all kinds of flowers.

The next morning when the intention of returning had prevailed over the opinion of tarrying, I saw that my friend had in his skirt collected roses,

[5] The second month of spring in the Iranian calendar.

'Night Banquet', unknown artist, Moraqqa'-e Golshan*, sixteenth century, Golestan Palace.*

sweet basil, hyacinths and fragrant herbs with the determination to carry them to town; whereon I said: 'Thou knowest that the roses of the garden are perishable and the season passes away', and philosophers have said: 'Whatever is not of long duration is not to be cherished.' He asked: 'Then what is to be done?' I replied: 'I may compose for the amusement of those who look and for the instruction of those who are present a book of a Rose Garden, a *Gulistan*, whose leaves cannot be touched by the tyranny of autumnal blasts and the delight of whose spring the vicissitudes of time will be unable to change into the inconstancy of autumn.'

Of what use will be a dish of roses to thee?
Take a leaf from my rose-garden.
A flower endures but five or six days
But this rose-garden is always delightful.

After I had uttered these words he threw away the flowers from his skirts, saying: 'When a generous fellow makes a promise he keeps it.'

On the same day I happened to write two chapters, namely on polite society and the rules of conversation, in a style acceptable to orators and instructive to letter-writers.

In short, some roses of the garden still remained when the book of the Rose-garden was finished.

A trained orator, old, aged,
First meditates and then speaks.
Do not speak without consideration.
Speak well and if slow what matters it?
Deliberate and then begin to talk.
Say thyself enough before others say enough.
By speech a man is better than a brute
But a beast is better unless thou speakest properly.

*

deliberation, then speech;
The foundation was laid first, then the wall.

Trusting in the liberal sentiments of the great, who shut their eyes to the faults of their inferiors and abstain from divulging the crimes of humble men, we have in this book recorded, by way of abridgment, some rare events, stories, poetry and accounts about ancient kings, spending a portion of our precious life in the task. This was the reason for composing the book *Gulistan*; and help is from Allah.

This well-arranged composition will remain for years,
When every atom of our dust is dispersed.
The intention of this design was that it should survive
Because I perceive no stability in my existence,
Unless one day a pious man compassionately
Utters a prayer for the works of dervishes.

The author, having deliberated upon the arrangement of the book, and the adornment of the chapters, deemed it suitable to curtail the diction of this beautiful garden and luxuriant grove and to make it resemble paradise, which also has eight entrances. The abridgment was made to avoid tediousness.

I. The Manners of Kings
II. On the Morals of Dervishes
III. On the Excellence of Content
IV. On the Advantages of Silence
V. On Love and Youth
VI. On Weakness and Old Age
VII. On the Effects of Education
VIII. On Rules for Conduct in Life

At a period when our time was pleasant
The Hejret[6] *was six hundred and fifty-six.*
Our intention was advice and we gave it.
We recommended thee to God and departed.

[6] It means migration and refers to the Islamic calendar, which began from the time of the Prophet Muhammad's migration.

Page from the 'Introductory' to Sa'di's Gulistan, *seventeenth century, Indo Iranian Album, Golestan Palace.*

CHAPTER 1

در سیرت پادشاهان

THE MANNERS OF KINGS

Story 1

I heard a padshah[7] giving orders to kill a prisoner. The helpless fellow began to insult the king on that occasion of despair, with the tongue he had, and to use foul expressions according to the saying:

Who washes his hands of life Says whatever he has in his heart.

In time of need, when flight is no more possible,
The hand grasps the point of the sharp sword.

•

When a man is in despair his tongue becomes long and he is
like a vanquished cat assailing a dog.

When the king asked what he was saying, a good-natured vazir[8] replied: 'My lord, he says:

Those who bridle their anger and forgive men; for Allah loveth the beneficent.'

The king, moved with pity, forbore taking his life but another vazir, the antagonist of the former, said: 'Men of our rank ought to speak nothing but the truth in the presence of padshahs. This fellow has insulted the king and spoken unbecomingly.'

The king, being displeased with these words, said: 'That lie was more acceptable to me than this truth thou hast uttered because the former proceeded from a conciliatory disposition and the latter from malignity; and wise men have said:'

[7] The king.
[8] The king's minister.

A FALSEHOOD RESULTING IN CONCILIATION IS BETTER THAN A TRUTH PRODUCING TROUBLE.

He whom the shah follows in what he says,
It is a pity if he speaks anything but what is good.

The following inscription was upon the portico of the hall of *Fereidun*[9]:

O brother, the world remains with no one.

Bind the heart to the Creator, it is enough.
Rely not upon possessions and this world
Because it has cherished many like thee and slain them.
When the pure soul is about to depart,
What boots it if one dies on a throne or on the ground?

Story 2

One of the kings of Khorasan had a vision in a dream of *Sultan Mahmud*[10] ... His whole person appeared to have been dissolved and turned to dust, except his eyes, which were revolving in their orbits and looking about. All the sages were unable to give an interpretation, except a dervish who made his salutation and said:

HE IS STILL LOOKING AMAZED HOW HIS KINGDOM BELONGS TO OTHERS.

Many famous men have been buried under ground
Of whose existence on earth not a trace has remained
And that old corpse which had been surrendered to the earth
Was so consumed by the soil that not a bone remains.
The glorious name of Nushirvan[11] *survives in good repute*
Although much time elapsed since he passed away.
Do good, O man, and consider life as a good fortune,
The more so, as when a shout is raised, a man exists no more.

[9] One of Iran's mythological kings, whose name appears in the *Shahnameh of Ferdowsi*.
[10] One of Iran's kings.
[11] One of Iran's kings.

Story 3

I have heard that a royal prince of short stature and mean presence, whose brothers were tall and good-looking, once saw his father glancing on him with aversion and contempt but he had the shrewdness and penetration to guess the meaning and said: 'O father, a puny intelligent fellow is better than a tall ignorant man.

NEITHER IS EVERYTHING BIGGER IN STATURE HIGHER IN PRICE.

•

A SHEEP IS NICE TO EAT AND AN ELEPHANT IS CARRION.

The smallest mountain on earth is Jur; nevertheless
It is great with Allah in dignity and station.

•

Hast thou not heard that a lean scholar
One day said to a fat fool:
"Although an Arab horse may be weak
It is thus more worth than a stable full of asses."'

The father laughed at this sally, the pillars of the state approved of it, but the brothers felt much aggrieved.

While a man says not a word
His fault and virtue are concealed
Think not that every desert is empty
Possibly it may contain a sleeping tiger.

I heard that on the said occasion the king was menaced by a powerful enemy and that when the two armies were about to encounter each other, the first who entered the battlefield was the little fellow who said:

'I am not he whose back thou wilt see on the day of battle
But he whom thou shalt behold in dust and blood.
Who himself fights, stakes his own life
In battle but he who flees, the blood of his army.'

After uttering these words he rushed among the troops of the enemy, slew several warriors and, returning to his father, made humble obeisance and said:

'O thou, to whom my person appeared contemptible,
Didst not believe in the impetuosity of my valour.
A horse with slender girth is of use
On the day of battle, not a fattened ox.'

It is related that the troops of the enemy were numerous, and that the king's, being few, were about to flee, but that the puny youth raised a shout, saying: 'O men, take care not to put on the garments of women.' These words augmented the rage of the troopers so that they made a unanimous attack and I heard that they gained the victory on the said occasion. The king kissed the head and eyes of his son, took him in his arms and daily augmented his affection till he appointed him to succeed him on the throne. His brothers became envious and placed poison in his food but were perceived by his sister from her apartment, whereon she closed the window violently and the youth, shrewdly guessing the significance of the act, restrained his hands from touching the food, and said:

IT IS IMPOSSIBLE THAT MEN OF HONOUR SHOULD DIE, AND THOSE WHO POSSESS NONE SHOULD TAKE THEIR PLACE.

No one goes under the shadow of an owl
Even if the homa should disappear from the world.

This state of affairs having been brought to the notice of the father, he severely reproved the brothers and assigned to each of them a different, but pleasant, district as a place of exile till the confusion was quelled and the quarrel appeased; and it has been said that:

TEN DERVISHES MAY SLEEP UNDER THE SAME BLANKET BUT THAT ONE COUNTRY CANNOT HOLD TWO PADSHAHS.

When a pious man eats half a loaf of bread
He bestows the other half upon dervishes.
If a padshah were to conquer the seven climates
He would still in the same way covet another.

Page from Sa'di's Bustan *(No. 2174), unknown artist, sixteenth century, Golestan Palace.*

Story 4

A band of Arab brigands having taken up their position on the top of a mountain and closed the passage of caravans, the inhabitants of the country were distressed by their stratagems and the troops of the sultan foiled because the robbers, having obtained an inaccessible spot on the summit of the mountain, thus had a refuge which they made their habitation. The chiefs of that region held a consultation about getting rid of the calamity because it would be impossible to offer resistance to the robbers if they were allowed to remain.

A tree which has just taken root
May be moved from the place by the strength of a man
But, if thou leavest it thus for a long time,
Thou canst not uproot it with a windlass.
The source of a fountain may be stopped with a bodkin
But, when it is full, it cannot be crossed on an elephant.

The conclusion was arrived at to send one man as a spy and to wait for the opportunity till the brigands departed to attack some people and leave the place empty. Then several experienced men, who had fought in battles, were despatched to keep themselves in ambush in a hollow of the mountain. In the evening the brigands returned from their excursion with their booty, divested themselves of their arms, put away their plunder and the first enemy who attacked them was sleep, till about a watch of the night had elapsed:

The disk of the sun went into darkness
Jonah went into the mouth of the fish.

The warriors leapt forth from the ambush, tied the hands of every one of the robbers to his shoulders and brought them in the morning to the court of the king, who ordered all of them to be slain. There happened to be a youth among them, the fruit of whose vigour was just ripening and the verdure on the rose-garden of whose cheek had begun to sprout. One of the vazirs, having kissed the foot of the king's throne and placed the face of intercession upon the ground, said: 'This boy has not yet eaten any fruit from the garden of life and has not yet enjoyed the pleasures of youth. I hope your majesty will generously and kindly confer an obligation upon your slave by sparing his life.' The king, being displeased with this request, answered:

He whose foundation is bad will not take instruction from the good,
To educate unworthy persons is like throwing nuts on a cupola.

'It is preferable to extirpate the race and offspring of these people and better to dig up their roots and foundations, because it is not the part of wise men to extinguish fire and to leave burning coals or to kill a viper and leave its young ones.'

If a cloud should rain the water of life
Never sip it from the branch of a willow-tree.
Associate not with a base fellow
Because thou canst not eat sugar from a mat-reed.

The vazir heard these sentiments, approved of them nolens volens, praised the opinion of the king and said: 'What my lord has uttered is the very truth itself because if the boy had been brought up in the company of those wicked men, he would have become one of themselves. But your slave hopes that he will, in the society of pious men, profit by education and will acquire the disposition of wise persons. Being yet a child the rebellious and perverse temper of that band has not yet taken hold of his nature.'

The spouse of Lot became a friend of wicked persons
His race of prophets became extinct.
The dog of the companions of the cave for some days
Associated with good people and became a man.

When the vazir had said these words and some of the courtiers had added their intercession to his, the king no longer desired to shed the blood of the youth and said: 'I grant the request although I disapprove of it.'

'Visit to a Dervish', signed Mahmud Muzahhib, Bukhara, 1560–61, Sa'di's Gulistan.

Knowest thou not what Zal said to the hero Rostam:
'An enemy cannot be held despicable or helpless.
I have seen many a water from a paltry spring
Becoming great and carrying off a camel with its load.'

In short, the vazir brought up the boy delicately, with every comfort, and kept masters to educate him, till they had taught him to address persons in elegant language as well as to reply and he had acquired every accomplishment. One day the vazir hinted at his talents in the presence of the king, asserting that the instructions of wise men had taken effect upon the boy and had expelled his previous ignorance from his nature. The king smiled at these words and said:

'At last a wolf's whelp will be a wolf
Although he may grow up with a man.'

After two years had elapsed a band of robbers in the locality joined him, tied the knot of friendship and, when the opportunity presented itself, he killed the vazir with his son, took away untold wealth and succeeded to the position of his own father in the robber-cave where he established himself. The king, informed of the event, took the finger of amazement between his teeth and said:

'How can a man fabricate a good sword of bad iron?
O sage, who is nobody becomes not somebody by education.
The rain, in the beneficence of whose nature there is no flaw,
Will cause tulips to grow in a garden and weeds in bad soil.

•

Saline earth will not produce hyacinths.
Throw not away thy seeds or work thereon.
To do good to wicked persons is like
Doing evil to good men.'

Story 5

It is narrated that one of the kings of Persia had stretched forth his tyrannical hand to the possessions of his subjects and had begun to oppress them so violently that in consequence of his fraudulent extortions they dispersed in the world and chose exile on account of the affliction entailed by his violence. When the population had diminished, the prosperity of the country suffered, the treasury remained empty and on every side enemies committed violence.

Who desires succour in the day of calamity,
Say to him: 'Be generous in times of prosperity.'
The slave with a ring in his ear, if not cherished will depart.
Be kind because then a stranger will become thy slave.

One day the *Shahnameh*[12] was read in his assembly, the subject being the ruin of the dominion of Zohak and the reign of Feridun. The vazir asked the king how it came to pass that Feridun, who possessed neither treasure nor land nor a retinue, established himself upon the throne. He replied: 'As thou hast heard, the population enthusiastically gathered around him and supported him so that he attained royalty.' The vazir said: 'As the gathering around of the population is the cause of royalty, then why dispersest thou the population? Perhaps thou hast no desire for royalty?'

It is best to cherish the army as thy life
Because a sultan reigns by means of his troops.

The king asked: 'What is the reason for the gathering around of the troops and the population?' He replied: 'A padshah must practise justice that they may gather around him and clemency that they may dwell in safety under the shadow of his government; but thou possessest neither of these qualities.'

[12] Its name means 'The Book of Kings', and it is the most important book in Persian literature and one of the greatest epics in the world.

A tyrannic man cannot be a sultan
As a wolf cannot be a shepherd.
A padshah who establishes oppression
Destroys the basis of the wall of his own reign.

The king, displeased with the advice of his censorious vazir, sent him to prison. Shortly afterwards the sons of the king's uncle rose in rebellion, desirous of recovering the kingdom of their father. The population, which had been reduced to the last extremity by the king's oppression and scattered, now assembled around them and supported them, till he lost control of the government and they took possession of it.

A padshah who allows his subjects to be oppressed
Will in his day of calamity become a violent foe.
Be at peace with subjects and sit safe from attacks of foes
Because his subjects are the army of a just shahanshah.

Story 6

A padshah was in the same boat with a Persian slave who had never before been at sea and experienced the inconvenience of a vessel. He began to cry and to tremble to such a degree that he could not be pacified by kindness, so that at last the king became displeased as the matter could not be remedied. In that boat there happened to be a philosopher, who said: 'With thy permission I shall quiet him.' The padshah replied: 'It will be a great favour.' The philosopher ordered the slave to be thrown into the water so that he swallowed some of it, whereon be was caught and pulled by his hair to the boat, to the stern of which he clung with both his hands. Then he sat down in a corner and became quiet. This appeared strange to the king who knew not what wisdom there was in the proceeding and asked for it. The philosopher replied: Before he had tasted the calamity of being drowned, he knew not the safety of the boat; thus also:

A MAN DOES NOT APPRECIATE THE VALUE OF IMMUNITY FROM A MISFORTUNE UNTIL IT HAS BEFALLEN HIM.

O thou full man, barley-bread pleases thee not.
She is my sweetheart who appears ugly to thee.
To the huris of paradise purgatory seems hell.
Ask the denizens of hell. To them purgatory is paradise.

•

There is a difference between him whose friend is in his arms
And him whose eyes of expectation are upon the door.

'The Flower and the Bird', Mohammad Yusof, seventeenth century, Indo Iranian Album, Golestan Palace.

Story 7

An Arab king was sick in his state of decrepitude so that all hopes of life were cut off. A trooper entered the gate with the good news that a certain fort had been conquered by the good luck of the king, that the enemies had been captured and that the whole population of the district had been reduced to obedience. The king heaved a deep sigh and replied: 'This message is not for me but for my enemies, namely the heirs of the kingdom.'

I spent my precious life in hopes, alas!
That every desire of my heart will be fulfilled.
My wishes were realized, but to what profit? Since
There is no hope that my past life will return.

•

The hand of fate has struck the drum of departure.
O my two eyes, bid farewell to the head.
O palm, forearm, and arm of my hand,
All take leave from each other.
Death, the foe of my desires, has fallen on me
For the last time, O friends. Pass near me.
My life has elapsed in ignorance.
I have done nothing, be on your guard.

Story 8

I was constantly engaged in prayer, at the head of the prophet Yahia's tomb in the cathedral mosque of Damascus, when one of the Arab kings, notorious for his injustice, happened to arrive on a pilgrimage to it, who offered his supplications and asked for compliance with his needs.

The dervish and the plutocrat are slaves on the floor of this threshold
And those who are the wealthiest are the most needy.

Then he said to me: 'Dervishes being zealous and veracious in their dealings, unite thy mind to mine, for I am apprehensive of a powerful enemy.' I replied:

'HAVE MERCY UPON THY FEEBLE SUBJECTS THAT THOU MAYEST NOT BE INJURED BY A STRONG FOE.'

With a powerful arm and the strength of the wrist
To break the five fingers of a poor man is sin.
Let him be afraid who spares not the fallen
Because if he falls no one will take hold of his hand.
Whoever sows bad seed and expects good fruit
Has cudgelled his brains for nought and begotten vain imaginations.
Extract the cotton from thy ears and administer justice to thy people
And if thou failest to do so, there is a day of retribution.

•

The sons of Adam are limbs of each other
Having been created of one essence.
When the calamity of time afflicts one limb
The other limbs cannot remain at rest.
If thou hast no sympathy for the troubles of others
Thou art unworthy to be called by the name of a man.

بنی آدم اعضای یکدیگرند
که در آفرینش ز یک گوهرند
چو عضوی به درد آورد روزگار
دگر عضوها را نماند قرار
تو کز محنت دیگران بی غمی
نشاید که نامت نهند آدمی

Story 9

An unjust king asked a devotee what kind of worship is best? He replied: 'For thee the best is to sleep one half of the day so as not to injure the people for a while.'

I saw a tyrant sleeping half the day.
I said: 'This confusion, if sleep removes it, so much the better;
But he whose sleep is better than his wakefulness
Is better dead than leading such a bad life.'

Page from Sa'di's Bustan *(No. 2197), unknown artist, 1553, Golestan Palace.*

Story 10

A vazir, who had been removed from his post, entered the circle of dervishes and the blessing of their society took such effect upon him that he became contented in his mind. When the king was again favourably disposed towards him and ordered him to resume his office, he refused and said: 'Retirement is better than occupation.'

Those who have sat down in the corner of safety
Have bound the teeth of dogs and tongues of men.
They tore the paper up and broke the pen
And are saved from the hands and tongues of slanderers.

The king said: 'Verily we stand in need of a man of sufficient intelligence who is able to carry on the administration of the government.' He replied: 'It is a sign of sufficient intelligence not to engage in such matters.'

The homa excels all other birds in nobility
Because it feeds on bones and injures no living thing.

A donkey, having been asked for what salary he had elected to attend upon the lion, replied: 'That I may consume the remnants of his prey and live in safety from my enemies by taking refuge under his bravery.' Being again asked that, as he had entered into the shadow of the lion's protection and gratefully acknowledged his beneficence, why he had not joined the circle of intimacy so as to be accounted one of his favourite servants, he replied: 'I am in the same way also not safe of his bravery.' It may happen that a companion of his majesty the sultan[13] receives gold and it is possible that he loses his head. Philosophers have said that:

IT IS NECESSARY TO BE ON GUARD OF THE FICKLE TEMPER OF PADSHAHS BECAUSE SOMETIMES THEY ARE DISPLEASED WITH POLITENESS AND AT OTHERS THEY BESTOW ROBES OF HONOUR FOR RUDENESS.

[13] King.

It is also said that much jocularity is an accomplishment in courtiers but a fault in sages.

Abide thou by thy dignity and gravity
Leave sport and jocularity to courtiers.

Story 11

One of my friends complained of the unpropitious times, telling me that he had a slender income, a large family, without strength to bear the load of poverty and had often entertained the idea to emigrate to another country so that no matter how he made a living no one might become aware of his good or ill luck.

Many a man slept hungry and no one knew who he was.
Many a man was at the point of death and no one wept for him.

He was also apprehensive of the malevolence of enemies who would laugh behind his back and would attribute the struggle he underwent for the benefit of his family to his want of manly independence and that they will say:

'Behold that dishonourable fellow who will never
See the face of prosperity,
Will choose bodily comfort for himself,
Abandoning his wife and children to misery.'

He also told me that as I knew he possessed some knowledge of arithmetic, I might, through my influence, get him appointed to a post which would become the means of putting his mind at ease and place him under obligations to me, which he could not requite by gratitude during the rest of his life. I replied: 'Dear friend!

EMPLOYMENT BY A PADSHAH CONSISTS OF TWO PARTS, NAMELY, THE HOPE FOR BREAD AND THE DANGER OF LIFE.

'Banquet of Homayoun and Akbar Shah', Abd-ol-Samad, Moraqqa'-e Golshan, *sixteenth century, Golestan Palace.*

But it is against the opinion of intelligent men to incur this danger for that hope.

No one comes to the house of a dervish
To levy a tax on land and garden.'

He replied: 'Thou hast not uttered these words in conformity with my case nor answered my question. Hast thou not heard the saying?

"WHOEVER COMMITS TREACHERY LET HIS HAND TREMBLE AT THE ACCOUNT."

Straightness is the means of acceptance with God.
I saw no one lost on the straight road.

Sages have said:

"FOUR PERSONS ARE FOR LIFE IN DREAD OF FOUR PERSONS: A ROBBER OF THE SULTAN, A THIEF OF THE WATCHMAN, AN ADULTERER OF AN INFORMER, AND A HARLOT OF THE MUHTASIB.[14]

But:

WHAT HAS HE TO FEAR WHOSE ACCOUNT OF THE CONSCIENCE IS CLEAR?"

Be not extravagant when in office, if thou desirest
On thy removal to see thy foes embarrassed for imputations against thee.
Be thou pure, O brother, and in fear of no one.
Washermen beat only impure garments against stones.'

I said: 'The story of that fox resembles thy case, who was by some persons seen fleeing with much trouble and asked for the cause of his fear replied: "I have heard that camels are being forced into the service." They said: "O fool, what connection hast thou with a camel and what resemblance does the latter bear to thee?" The fox rejoined: "Hush. If the envious malevolently say that I am a camel and I am caught, who will care to release me or investigate my case?"

[14] Inspector.

Till the antidote is brought from Eraq
the snake-bitten person dies.

Thou art a very excellent and honest man but enemies sit in ambush and competitors in every corner. If they describe thy character in a contrary manner, thou wouldst be called upon to give explanations to the padshah and incur reproof. Who would on that occasion venture to say anything? Accordingly I am of opinion that thou shouldst retire to the domain of contentment and abandon aspirations to dominion.

"In the sea there are countless gains,
But if thou desirest safety, it will be on the shore."'

My friend, having heard these words, became angry, made a wry face and began to reproach me, saying: 'What sufficiency of wisdom and maturity of intellect is this? The saying of philosophers has come true, that friends are useful in prison because at table all enemies appear as friends.'

Account him not a friend who knocks at the door of prosperity,
Boasts of amity and calls himself thy adopted brother.
I consider him a friend who takes a friend's hand
When he is in a distressed state and in poverty.

Seeing that he had thus changed and ascribed my advice to an interested motive, I paid a visit to the President of the State Council and, trusting in my old acquaintance with him, explained the case of my friend whom he then appointed to a small post. In a short time my friend's affable behaviour and good management elicited approbation so that he was promoted to a higher office. In this manner the star of his good luck ascended till he reached the zenith of his aspirations, became a courtier of his majesty the sultan, generally esteemed and trusted. I was delighted with his safe position and said:

'Be not apprehensive of tangled affairs and keep not a broken heart
Because the spring of life is in darkness.'
Do not grieve, O brother in misery,

'Tadhib', unknown artist, Moraqqa'-e Golshan, *seventeenth century, Golestan Palace.*

Because the Ill-merciful has hidden favours.
Sit not morose on account of the turns of time; for patience,
Although bitter, nevertheless possesses a sweet fruit.

At that time I happened to go with a company of friends on a journey to Mekkah and on my return he met me at a distance of two stages. I perceived his outward appearance to be distressed, his costume being that of dervishes. I asked: 'What is the matter?' He replied: 'As thou hast predicted, some persons envied me and brought against me an accusation of treason. The king ordered no inquiry on its truthfulness and my old well-wishers with my kind friends who failed to speak the word of truth forgot our old intimacy.

Seest thou not in front of the possessor of dignity
They place the hands on their heads, praising him;
But, if fortune's turn causes his fall,
All desire to Place their foot on his head.

In short, I was till this week undergoing various persecutions, when the news of the pilgrims' approach from Mekkah arrived, whereon I was released from my heavy bonds and my hereditary property confiscated.' I replied: 'Thou hast not paid attention to my remarks when I said that the service of padshahs is like a sea voyage, profitable and dangerous, so that thou wilt either gain a treasure or perish in the waves.'

The khajah either takes gold with both hands to the shore
Or the waves throw him one day dead upon the shore.

Not thinking it suitable to scratch the wound of the dervish more than I had already done and so sprinkle salt thereon, I contented myself with reciting the following two distichs:

Knewest thou not that thou wilt see thy feet in bonds
If the advice of people cannot penetrate into thy ear?
Again, if thou canst not bear the pain of the sting
Put not thy finger into the hole of a scorpion.

Story 12

It is related that, whilst some game was being roasted for *Nushirvan*[15] the just during a hunting party, no salt could be found. Accordingly a boy was sent to an adjoining village to bring some. Nushirvan said: 'Pay for the salt lest it should become a custom and the village be ruined.' Having been asked what harm could arise from such a trifling demand, Nushirvan replied:

THE FOUNDATION OF OPPRESSION WAS SMALL IN THE WORLD
BUT WHOEVER CAME AUGMENTED IT SO THAT IT REACHED
ITS PRESENT MAGNITUDE.

If the king eats one apple from the garden of a subject
His slaves will pull him up the tree from the roots.
For five eggs which the sultan allows to be taken by force
The people belonging to his army will put a thousand fowls on the spit.

[15] One of Iran's kings.

Story 13

I heard that an oppressor ruined the habitations of the subjects to fill the treasury of the sultan, unmindful of the maxim of philosophers, who have said: 'Who offends God the most high to gain the heart of a created being, God will use that very being to bring on his destruction in the world.'

Fire burning with wild rue will not
Cause a smoke like that of afflicted hearts.

The prince of all animals is the lion and the meanest of beasts the ass. Nevertheless sages agree that:

An ass who carries loads is better than
a lion who destroys men.

The poor donkey though void of discernment
Is nevertheless esteemed when he carries a burden.
Oxen and asses who carry loads
Are superior to men oppressing mankind.

When the king had obtained information of some of the oppressor's misdeeds and bad conduct, he had him put on the rack and slain by various tortures.

Thou wilt not obtain the approbation of the sultan
Unless thou seekest the goodwill of his subjects.
If thou desirest God to condone thy transgressions,
Do good to the people whom God has created.

One of the oppressed who passed near him said:

'Not everyone who possesses strength of arm and office
In the sultanate may with impunity plunder the people.

A hard bone may be made to pass down the throat
But it will tear the belly when it sticks in the navel.'

•

A tyrant does not remain in the world
But the curse on him abides for ever.

Story 14

It is narrated that an oppressor of the people, a soldier, hit the head of a pious man with a stone and that the dervish, having no means of taking vengeance, preserved the stone till the time arrived when the king became angry with that soldier, and imprisoned him in a well. Then the dervish made his appearance and dropped the stone upon his head. He asked: 'Who art thou, and why hast thou hit my head with this stone?' The man replied: 'I am the same person whom thou hast struck on the head with this stone on such and such a day.' The soldier continued: 'Where hast thou been all this time?' The dervish replied: 'I was afraid of thy dignity but now when I beheld thee in the well I made use of the opportunity.'

When thou seest an unworthy man in good luck
Intelligent men have chosen submission.
If thou hast not a tearing sharp nail
It will be better not to contend with the wicked.
Who grasps with his fist one who has an arm of steel
Injures only his own powerless wrist.
Wait till inconstant fortune ties his hand.
Then, to please thy friends, pick out his brains.

'Court Banquet', Aqa Reza, Moraqqa'-e Golshan *(p. 131), sixteenth century, Golestan Palace.*

Story 15

A king was subject to a terrible disease, the mention of which is not sanctioned by custom. The tribe of Yunani physicians agreed that this pain cannot be allayed except by means of the bile of a person endued with certain qualities. Orders having been issued to search for an individual of this kind, the son of a landholder was discovered to possess the qualities mentioned by the doctors. The king summoned the father and mother of the boy whose consent he obtained by giving them immense wealth. The qazi[16] issued a judicial decree that it is permissible to shed the blood of one subject for the safety of the king and the executioner was ready to slay the boy who then looked heavenwards and smiled. The king asked: 'What occasion for laughter is there in such a position?' The youth replied: 'A son looks to the affection of his father and mother to bring his case before the qazi and to ask justice from the padshah. In the present instance, however, the father and mother have for the trash of this world surrendered my blood, the qazi has issued a decree to kill me, the sultan thinks he will recover his health only through my destruction and I see no other refuge besides God the most high.'

To whom shall I complain against thy hand
If I am to seek justice also from thy hand?

The sultan became troubled at these words, tears rushed to his eyes and he said: 'It is better for me to perish than to shed innocent blood.' He kissed the head and eyes of the youth, presented him with boundless wealth and it is said that the king also recovered his health during that week.

I also remember the distich recited
By the elephant-driver on the bank of the Nile:
'If thou knewest the state of the ant under thy foot
It is like thy own condition under the foot of an elephant.'

[16] Judge.

Story 16

King of Zuzan had a khajah[17] of noble sentiments and of good aspect who served his companions when they were present and spoke well of them when they were absent. He happened to do something whereby he incurred the displeasure of the king who inflicted a fine on him and also otherwise punished him. The officials of the king, mindful of the benefits they had formerly received from him and being by them pledged to gratitude, treated him kindly whilst in their custody and allowed no one to insult him.

If thou desirest peace from the foe, whenever he
Finds fault behind thy back praise him to his face.
A vicious fellow's mouth must utter words.
If thou desirest not bitter words, sweeten his mouth.

He was absolved of some accusations brought by the king against him but retained in prison for some. Another king in those regions secretly dispatched a message to him, to the purport that the sovereigns of that country, not knowing his excellent qualities, had dishonoured him, but that if his precious mind (may Allah prosper the end of his affairs) were to look in this direction, the utmost efforts would be made to please him, because the nobles of this realm would consider it an honour to see him and are waiting for a reply to this letter. The khajah, who had received this information, being apprehensive of danger, forthwith wrote a brief and suitable answer on the back of the sheet of paper and sent it back. One, however, of the king's courtiers, who noticed what had taken place, reported to him that the imprisoned khajah was in correspondence with the princes of the adjacent country. The king became angry and desired this affair to be investigated.

The courier was overtaken and deprived of the letter, the contents of which were found on perusal to be as follows: 'The good opinion of high personages is more than their servant's merit deserves, who is unable to comply with the honour of reception which they have offered him,

[17] The king's minister or one of the courtiers or king's companions.

because having been nourished by the bounty of this dynasty, he cannot become unthankful towards his benefactor in consequence of a slight change of sentiments of the latter, since it is said:

He who bestows every moment favours upon thee
Is to be pardoned by thee if once in his life he injures thee.'

The king approved of his gratitude, bestowed upon him a robe of honour, gave him presents and asked his pardon, saying: 'I committed a mistake.' He replied: 'My lord, it was the decree of God the most high that a misfortune should befall this servant but it was best that it should come from thy hands which had formerly bestowed favours upon him and placed him under obligations.'

If people injure thee grieve not
Because neither rest nor grief come from the people.
Be aware that the contrasts of friend and foe are from God
Because the hearts of both are in his keeping.
Although the arrow is shot from the bow
Wise men look at the archer.

'Gathering in Nature', unknown artist, seventeenth century, Indo Iranian Album, Golestan Palace.

Story 17

It is narrated that a tyrant who purchased wood from dervishes forcibly gave it away to rich people gratuitously. A pious man passing near said:

'Thou art a snake, stingest whom thou beholdest,
Or an owl; wherever thou sittest thou destroyest.

•

Although thy oppression may pass among us
It cannot pass with the Lord who knows all secrets.
Oppress not the denizens of the earth
That their supplications may not pass to heaven.'

The tyrant, being displeased with these words, got angry and took no notice of him until one night, when fire from the kitchen fell into the store of his wood and burnt all he possessed – transferring him from his soft bed to a hot mound of ashes – the same pious man happened again to pass and to hear him saying to his friends: 'I do not know whence this fire has fallen into my house.' He replied: 'From the smoke of the hearts of dervishes.'

Beware of the smoke of internal wounds
Because at last an internal wound will break out.
Forbear to uproot one heart as long as thou canst
Because one sigh may uproot a world.

Upon the diadem of *Kaikhosru*[18] the following piece was inscribed:

For how many years and long lives
Will the people walk over my head on the ground?
As from hand to hand the kingdom came to us
So it will also go to other hands.

[18] One of Iran's mythological kings, whose name appears in the *Shahnameh* of Ferdowsi.

Story 18

A man had attained great excellence in the art of wrestling, who knew three hundred and sixty exquisite tricks and daily exhibited something new. He had a particular affection for the beauty of one of his pupils whom he taught three hundred and fifty-nine tricks, refraining to impart to him only one. At last the youth had attained such power and skill that no one was able to contend with him and he went so far as to say to the sultan: 'I allow superiority to my teacher on account of his age and from gratitude for his instruction but my strength is not less than his and my skill equal.'

The king, who was not pleased with this want of good manners, ordered them to wrestle with each other and a spacious locality having been fixed upon, the pillars of state and courtiers of his majesty made their appearance. The youth made an onslaught like a mad elephant with an impulse which might have uprooted a mountain of brass from its place but the master, who knew that he was in strength superior to himself, attacked him with the rare trick he had reserved to himself and which the youth was unable to elude; whereon the master, lifting him up with his hands from the ground, raised him above his head and then threw him down.

Shouts were raised by the spectators and the king ordered a robe of honour with other presents to be given to the teacher but reproached and blamed the youth for having attempted to cope with his instructor and succumbed.

He replied: 'My lord, he has not vanquished me by his strength but there was a slender part in the art of wrestling which he had withheld from me and had today thereby got the upper hand of me.' The master said: 'I had reserved it for such an occasion because wise men have said:

"Do not give so much strength to thy friend that, if he becomes thy foe, he may injure thee."

Hast thou not heard what the man said who suffered molestation from one whom he had educated?

Either fidelity itself does not exist in this world
Or nobody practices it in our time.
No one had learnt archery from me
Without at last making a target of me.'

From Sa'di's Bustan, *unknown artist, 1553, Golestan Palace.*

Story 19

A solitary dervish was sitting in a corner of the desert when a padshah happened to pass by but, ease having made him independent, he took no notice. The sultan, in conformity with his royal dignity, became angry and said: 'This tribe of rag-wearers resembles beasts.' The vazir said: 'The padshah of the surface of the earth has passed near thee. Why hast thou not paid homage and shown good manners?' He replied: 'Tell the king to look for homage from a man who expects benefits from him and also that:

KINGS EXIST FOR PROTECTING SUBJECTS AND SUBJECTS NOT FOR OBEYING KINGS.'

The padshah is the guardian of the dervish
Although wealth is in the glory of his reign.
The sheep is not for the shepherd
But the shepherd for the service of it.

•

Today thou beholdest one man prosperous
And another whose heart is wounded by struggling.
Wait a few days till the earth consumes
The brain in the head of the visionary.
Distinction between king and slave has ceased
When the decree of fate overtakes them.
If a man were to open the tombs of the dead
He would not distinguish a rich from a poor man.

The king, who was pleased with the sentiments of the dervish, asked him to make a request but he answered that the only one he had to make was to be left alone. The king then asked for advice and the dervish said:

'Understand now while wealth is in thy hand
That fortune and kingdom will leave thy hand.'

Story 20

A vazir paid a visit to *Zulnun Misri*[19] and asked for his favour, saying:
'I am day and night engaged in the service of the sultan and hoping to be rewarded but nevertheless dread to be punished by him.' Zulnun wept and said: 'Had I feared God, the great and glorious, as thou fearest the sultan, I would be one of the number of the righteous.'

If there were no hope of rest and trouble
The foot of the dervish would be upon the sphere
And if the vazir feared God
Like the king he would be king.

Story 21

A padshah having issued orders to kill an innocent man, the latter said: 'O king, seek not thine own injury on account of the anger thou bearest towards me.' He asked: 'How?' The man replied: 'This punishment will abide with me one moment but the sin of it for ever with thee.'

The period of life has passed away like the desert wind.
Bitter and sweet, ugliness and beauty have passed away.
The tyrant found he had done injury to us.
It remained on his neck and passed away from us.

This admonition having taken effect, the king spared his blood.

[19] One of the famous mystics, whose name appears in the *Tazkirat al-Awliya (Biographies of the Saints) of Attar.*

'Farewell of Comrades', unknown artist, Sa'di's Bustan and Gulistan, *Reza Abbasi Museum.*

Story 22

One of the vazirs treated his subordinates with kindness and sought their goodwill. Once he happened to be called to account by the king for something he had done whereon his colleagues endeavoured to effect his liberation. Those who guarded him treated him leniently and the great men expatiated upon his good character to the padshah till he renounced all further inquiry. A pious man who took cognizance of this affair said:

'In order to gain the hearts of friends
Sell even the garden of thy father.
In order to boil the pot of well-wishers
Burn even all the furniture of the house.
Do good even to a malevolent fellow.
Tie up the mouth of the dog with a sop.'

Story 23

I was sitting in a vessel with a company of great men when a boat which contained two brothers happened to sink near us. One of the great men promised a hundred dinars to a sailor if he could save them both. Whilst however the sailor was pulling out one, the other perished. I said: 'He had no longer to live and therefore delay took place in rescuing him.' The sailor smiled and replied: 'What thou hast said is certain. Moreover, I preferred to save this one because, when I once-happened to lag behind in the desert, he seated me on his camel, whereas I had received a whipping by the hands of the other. When I was a boy I recited:

He, who doth right, doth it to his own soul and he, who doth evil, doth it against the same.'

As long as thou canst, scratch the interior of no one
Because there are thorns on this road.
Be helpful in the affairs of a dervish
Because thou also hast affairs.

Story 24

There were two brothers: one of them in the service of the sultan and the other gaining his livelihood by the effort of his arm. The wealthy man once asked his destitute brother why he did not serve the sultan in order to be delivered from the hardship of labouring. He replied: 'Why labourest thou not to be delivered from the baseness of service because philosophers have said that:

IT IS BETTER TO EAT BARLEY BREAD AND TO SIT THAN TO GIRD ONESELF WITH A GOLDEN BELT AND TO STAND IN SERVICE.

To leaven mortar of quicklime with the hand
Is better than to hold them on the breast before the amir.

•

My precious life was spent in considering
What I am to eat in summer and wear in winter.
O ignoble belly, be satisfied with one bread
Rather than to bend the back in service.

Story 25

Someone had brought information to *Nushirvan*[20] the just that an enemy of his had been removed from this world by God the most high. He asked: 'Hast thou heard anything about his intending to spare me?'

There is no occasion for our rejoicing at a foe's death
Because our own life will also not last for ever.

[20] One of Iran's kings.

Story 26

A company of philosophers were discussing a subject in the palace of *Kesra*[21] and *Bozorgmehr*[22], having remained silent, they asked him why he took no share in the debate. He replied:

'VAZIRS ARE LIKE PHYSICIANS AND THE LATTER GIVE MEDICINE TO THE SICK ONLY.

But, as I perceive that your opinions are in conformity with propriety, I have nothing to say about them.'

When an affair succeeds without my idle talk
It is not meet for me to speak thereon.
But if I see a blind man near a well
It is a crime for me to remain silent.

Two verses from Sa'di's Gulistan, *calligraphy by Mir Ali Heravi, sixteenth century.*

[21] One of Iran's kings.
[22] One of the famous ministers and sages in Iranian history.

'Dancing of Abed's Camel', unknown artist, Sa'di's Gulistan *(No. 2161), sixteenth century, Golestan Palace.*

باب دوم

CHAPTER 2

در اخلاق درویشان

THE MORALS OF DERVISHES

Story 1

One of the great devotees having been asked about his opinion concerning a hermit whom others had censured in their conversation, he replied: 'I do not see any external blemishes on him and do not know of internal ones.'

Whomsoever thou seest in a religious habit
Consider him to be a religious and good man
And, if thou knowest not his internal condition,
What business has the muhtasib inside the house?

Story 2

A thief paid a visit to the house of a pious man but, although he sought a great deal, found nothing and was much grieved. The pious man, who knew this, threw the blanket upon which he had been sleeping into the way of the thief that he might not go away disappointed.

I heard that men of the way of God
Have not distressed the hearts of enemies.
How canst thou attain that dignity
Who quarrelest and wagest war against friends?

The friendship of pure men, whether in thy presence or absence, is not such as will find fault behind thy back and is ready to die for thee before thy face.

In thy presence gentle like a lamb,
In thy absence like a man-devouring wolf.

*

Who brings the faults of another to thee and enumerates them
Will undoubtedly carry thy faults to others.

Story 3

A hermit, being the guest of a padshah, ate less than he wished when sitting at dinner and when he rose for prayers he prolonged them more than was his wont in order to enhance the opinion entertained by the padshah of his piety.

O Arab of the desert, I fear thou wilt not reach the Ka'bah
Because the road on which thou travellest leads to Turkestan.

When he returned to his own house, he desired the table to be laid out for eating. He had an intelligent son who said: 'Father, hast thou not eaten anything at the repast of the sultan?' He replied: 'I have not eaten anything to serve a purpose.' The boy said: 'Then likewise say thy prayers again as thou hast not done anything to serve that purpose.'

O thou who showest virtues on the palms of the hand
But concealest thy errors under the armpit
What wilt thou purchase, O vain-glorious fool,
On the day of distress with counterfeit silver?

Story 4

I remember, being in my childhood pious, rising in the night, addicted to devotion and abstinence. One night I was sitting with my father, remaining awake and holding the beloved Quran in my lap, whilst the people around us were asleep. I said: 'Not one of these persons lifts up his head or makes a genuflection. They are as fast asleep as if they were dead.' He replied: 'Darling of thy father, would that thou wert also asleep rather than disparaging people.'

The pretender sees no one but himself
Because he has the veil of conceit in front.
If he were endowed with a God-discerning eye
He would see that no one is weaker than himself.

Page from Sa'di's Bustan *(K.S. 582), unknown artist, seventeenth century, Reza Abbasi Museum.*

Story 5

A great man was praised in an assembly and, his good qualities being extolled, he raised his head and said: 'I am such as I know myself to be.'

O thou who reckonest my virtues, refrainest from giving me pain,
These are my open, and thou knowest not my hidden, qualities.

•

My person is, to the eyes of the world, of good aspect
But my internal wickedness makes me droop my head with shame.
The peacock is for his beauteous colours by the people
Praised whilst he is ashamed of his ugly feet.

'Alexander Crosses the Sea of China', unknown artist, Eskandar Name of Nezami *(No. 2222), Golestan Palace.*

Story 6

I spoke in the cathedral mosque of Damascus a few words by way of a sermon but to a congregation whose hearts were withered and dead, not having travelled from the road of the world of form, the physical, to the world of meaning, the moral world. I perceived that my words took no effect and that burning fire does not kindle moist wood. I was sorry for instructing brutes and holding forth a mirror in a locality of blind people. I had, however, opened the door of meaning and was giving a long explanation of the verse We are nearer unto Him than the jugular vein till I said:

'The Friend is nearer to me than my self,
But it is more strange that I am far from him.
What am I to do? To whom can it be said that he
Is in my arms, but I am exiled from him.'

I had intoxicated myself with the wine of these sentiments, holding the remnant of the cup of the sermon in my hand when a traveller happened to pass near the edge of the assembly, and the last turn of the circulating cup made such an impression upon him that he shouted and the others joined him who began to roar, whilst the raw portion of the congregation became turbulent. Whereon I said: 'Praise be to Allah! Those who are far away but intelligent are in the presence of Allah, and those who are near but blind are distant.'

When the hearer understands not the meaning of words
Do not look for the effect of the orator's force
But raise an extensive field of desire
That the eloquent man may strike the ball of effect.

Story 7

A dervish who had fallen into want stole a blanket from the house of a friend. The judge ordered his hand to be amputated but the owner of the blanket interceded, saying that he had condoned the fault. The judge rejoined: 'Thy intercession cannot persuade me to neglect the provision of the law.' The man continued: 'Thou hast spoken the truth but amputation is not applicable to a person who steals some property dedicated to pious uses. Moreover a beggar possesses nothing and whatever belongs to a dervish is dedicated to the use of the needy.' Thereon the judge released the culprit, saying: 'The world must indeed have become too narrow for thee that thou hast committed no theft except from the house of such a friend.' He replied: 'Hast thou not heard the saying:

SWEEP OUT THE HOUSE OF FRIENDS AND DO NOT KNOCK AT THE DOOR OF FOES.

If thou sinkest in a calamity be not helpless.
Strip thy foes of their skins and thy friends of their fur-coats.'

Story 8

A padshah, meeting a holy man, asked him whether he did not sometimes remember him for the purpose of getting presents. He replied: 'Yes, I do, whenever I forget God.'

Whom He drives from his door, runs everywhere.
Whom He calls, runs to no one's door.

Story 9

A bareheaded and barefooted pedestrian who had arrived from Kufah with the Hejaz-caravan of pilgrims joined us, strutted about and recited:

'I am neither riding a camel nor under a load like a camel.
I am neither a lord of subjects nor the slave of a potentate.
Grief for the present, or distress for the past, does not trouble me.
I draw my breath in comfort and thus spend my life.'

A camel-rider shouted to him: 'O dervish, where art thou going? Return, for thou wilt expire from hardships.' He paid no attention but entered the desert and marched. When we reached the station at the palm-grove of Mahmud, the rich man was on the point of death and the dervish, approaching his pillow, said: 'We have not expired from hardship but thou hast died on a dromedary.'

A man wept all night near the head of a patient.
When the day dawned he died and the patient revived.

•

Many a fleet charger had fallen dead
While a lame ass reached the station alive.
Often healthy persons were in the soil
Buried and the wounded did not die.

Story 10

A hermit, having been invited by a padshah, concluded that if he were to take some medicine to make himself weak he might perhaps enhance the opinion of the padshah regarding his merits. But it is related that the medicine was lethal so that when he partook of it he died.

Who appeared to thee all marrow like a pistachio
Was but skin upon skin like an onion.
Devotees with their face towards the world
Say their prayers with their back to the Qiblah.

•

When a worshipper calls upon his God,
He must know no one besides God.

Story 11

A caravan having been plundered in the Yunan country and deprived of boundless wealth, the merchants wept and lamented, beseeching God and the prophet to intercede for them with the robbers, but ineffectually.

When a dark-minded robber is victorious
What cares he for the weeping of the caravan?

Loqman[23] the Wise[24] being among the people of the caravan, one of them asked him to speak a few words of wisdom and advice to the robbers so that they might perhaps return some of the property they had plundered because the loss of so much wealth would be lamentable. *Loqman* replied: 'It would be lamentable to utter one word of wisdom to them.'

The rust which has eaten into iron
Cannot be removed by polishing.
Of what use is preaching to a black heart?
An iron nail cannot be driven into a rock.

•

Help the distressed in the day of prosperity
Because comforting the poor averts evil from thyself.
When a mendicant implores thee for a thing,
Give it or else an oppressor may take it by force.

[23] One of the sages of the ancient world.
[24] Originally translated as: Loqman the Philosopher.

Story 12

Loqman, being asked from whom he had learnt civility, replied: 'From those who had no civility because what appeared to me unbecoming in them I refrained from doing.'

Not a word is said even in sport
Without an intelligent man taking advice thereby.
But if a hundred chapters of wisdom are read to a fool
All strike his ear merely as sport.

Tadhib, unknown artist, Nezami's Khamseh, 1536 AD.

Story 13

It is related that a hermit consumed during one night ten mann of food and perused the whole Quran till morning. A pious fellow who had heard of this said: 'It would have been more excellent if he had eaten half a loaf and slept till the morning.'

Keep thy interior empty of food
That thou mayest behold therein the light of marifet.
Thou art empty of wisdom for the reason
That thou art replete with food up to the nose.

Story 14

A man had by his sins forfeited the divine favour but the lamp of grace nevertheless so shone upon his path that it guided him into the circle of religious men and, by the blessing of his association with dervishes, as well as by the example of their righteousness, the depravities of his character were transmuted into virtues and he refrained from lust and passion. But the tongues of the malevolent were lengthened with reference to his character, alleging that it was the same as it had ever been and that his abstinence and piety were spurious.

By apology and penitence one may be saved from the wrath of
God but cannot be saved from the tongues of men.

He could no longer bear the reviling tongues and complained to the pir of the Tariqat. The sheikh wept and said: 'How wilt thou be able to be sufficiently grateful for this divine favour that thou art better than the people imagine?'

How long wilt thou say: 'The malevolent and envious
Are searching out the defects of my humble self.
Sometimes they arise to shed my blood.

Sometimes they sit down to curse me.'
To be good and to be spoken of by the people
Is better than to be bad and considered good by them.

Look at me whom the good opinion of our contemporaries deems to be perfect whereas I am imperfection itself.

If I were doing what I speak
I would be of good conduct and a devotee.

•

Verily I am veiled from the eyes of my neighbours
But Allah knows my secret and my overt concerns.

•

The door is locked to the access of people
That they may not spread out my faults.
What profiteth a closed door?
The Omniscient Knows what I conceal or reveal.

Story 15

I COMPLAINED TO ONE OF THE SHEIKHS THAT A CERTAIN MAN HAD FALSELY ACCUSED ME OF LASCIVIOUSNESS. HE REPLIED: 'PUT HIM TO SHAME BY THY GOOD CONDUCT.'

Be thou well behaved that a maligner
May not find occasion to speak of thy faults.
When the barbat[25] *is in proper tune*
How can the hand of the musician correct it?

[25] Lute.

Story 16

One of the sheikhs of Syria, being asked on the true state of the Sufis, replied: 'In former times they were a tribe in the world, apparently distressed, but in reality contented whereas today they are people outwardly satisfied but inwardly discontented.'

If my heart roams away from thee every hour,
Thou wilt find no tranquillity in solitude
But if thou possessest property, dignity, fields and wares,
If thy heart be with God, thou wilt be a recluse.

'The Story of the Pious Camel', unknown artist, Sa'di's Bustan and Gulistan, *Reza Abbasi Museum.*

Story 17

I remember having once walked all night with a caravan and then slept on the edge of the desert. A distracted man who had accompanied us on that journey raised a shout, ran towards the desert and took not a moment's rest. When it was daylight, I asked him what state of his that was. He replied: 'I saw bulbuls commencing to lament on the trees, the partridges on the mountains, the frogs in the water and the beasts in the desert so I bethought myself that it would not be becoming for me to sleep in carelessness while they all were praising God.'

Yesterday at dawn a bird lamented,
Depriving me of sense, patience, strength and consciousness.
One of my intimate friends who
Had perhaps heard my distressed voice
Said: 'I could not believe that thou
Wouldst be so dazed by a bird's cry.'
I replied: 'It is not becoming to humanity
That I should be silent when birds chant praises.'

Story 18

It once happened that on a journey to the Hejaz a company of young and pious men, whose sentiments harmonized with mine, were my fellow-travellers. They occasionally sung and recited spiritual verses but we had with us also an a'bid, who entertained a bad opinion of the behaviour of the dervishes and was ignorant of their sufferings. When we reached the palm-grove of the Beni Hallal, a black boy of the encampment, falling into a state of excitement, broke out in a strain which brought down the birds from the sky. I saw, however, the camel of the a'bid, which began to prance, throwing him and running into the desert.

لقمان را گفتند: ادب از که آموختی؟ گفت: از بی ادبان. هرچه از ایشان در نظرم ناپسند آمد، از فعل آن پرهیز کردم.

Knowest thou what that matutinal bulbul said to me?
What man art thou to be ignorant of love?
The Arabic verses threw a camel into ecstasy and joy.
If thou hast no taste thou art an ill-natured brute.

•

When the winds blow over the plain
The branches of the ban-tree bend, not hard rocks.

•

Whatever thou beholdest chants his praises.
He knows this who has the true perception.
Not only the bulbul on the rosebush sings praises
But every bramble is a tongue, extolling him.

Story 19

The life of a king was drawing to a close and he had no successor. He ordered in his last testament that the next morning after his death the first person entering the gate of the city be presented with the royal crown and be entrusted with the government of the realm. It so happened that the first person who entered was a mendicant who had all his life subsisted on the morsels he collected and had sewn patch after patch upon his clothes. The pillars of the state and grandees of the court executed the injunction of the king and bestowed upon him the government and the treasures; whereon the dervish reigned for a while until some amirs of the monarchy withdrew their necks from his obedience and kings from every side began to rise for hostilities and to prepare their armies for war. At last his own troops and subjects also rebelled and deprived him of a portion of his dominions.

This event afflicted the mind of the dervish until one of his old friends, who had been his companion when he was yet himself a dervish, returned from a journey and, seeing him in such an exalted position, said: 'Thanks be to God the most high and glorious that thy rose has thus come forth from the thorn and thy thorn was extracted from thy foot. Thy high luck has aided thee and prosperity with fortune has guided thee till thou hast attained this position. Verily hardship is followed by comfort.'

A flower is sometimes blooming and sometimes withering.
A tree is at times nude and at times clothed.

He replied: 'Brother, condole with me because there is no occasion for congratulation. When thou sawest me last, I was distressed for bread and now a world of distress has overwhelmed me.'

If I have no wealth I grieve.
If I have some the love of it captivates me.
There is no greater calamity than worldly goods.
Both their possession and their want are griefs.

•

If thou wishest for power, covet nothing
Except contentment which is sufficient happiness.
If a rich man pours gold into thy lap
Care not a moment for thanking him.
Because often I heard great men say
The patience of a dervish is better than the gift of a rich man.

Story 20

Having become tired of my friends in Damascus, I went into the desert of Jerusalem and associated with animals till the time when I became a prisoner of the Franks, who put me to work with infidels in digging the earth of a moat in Tarapolis, when one of the chiefs of Aleppo, with whom I had formerly been acquainted, recognized me and said: 'What state is this?' I recited:

'I fled from men to mountain and desert
Wishing to attend upon no one but God.
Imagine what my state at present is
When I must be satisfied in a stable of wretches.

•

The feet in chains with friends
Is better than to be with strangers in a garden.'

He took pity on my state and ransomed me for ten dinars from the captivity of the Franks, taking me to Aleppo where he had a daughter and married me to her with a dowry of one hundred dinars. After some time had elapsed, she turned out to be ill-humoured, quarrelsome, disobedient, abusive in her tongue and embittering my life:

A bad wife in a good man's house
Is his hell in this world already.

Once she lengthened her tongue of reproach and said: 'Art thou not the man whom my father purchased from the Franks for ten dinars?' I replied: 'Yes, he bought me for ten dinars and sold me into thy hands for one hundred dinars.'

I heard that a sheep had by a great man
Been rescued from the jaws and the power of a wolf.
In the evening he stroked her throat with a knife
Whereon the soul of the sheep complained thus:
'Thou hast snatched me away from the claws of a wolf,
But at last I see thou art thyself a wolf.'

Story 21

An affair of importance emerged to a padshah, who thereon vowed that, if it terminated according to his wishes, he would present devotees with a certain sum of money. His wish having been fulfilled, it became necessary to keep his promise. Accordingly he gave a purse of dirhems to one of his confidential servants to distribute it among recluses.

It is related that the slave was intelligent and shrewd. He walked about all day and returning at nightfall, kissed the dirhems and deposited them before the king with the remark that he had not found any devotees. The king rejoined: 'What nonsense is this? As far as I know there are four hundred devotees in this town.' He said: 'Lord of the world, who is a devotee does not accept money and who accepts it is not a devotee.' The king smiled and said to his courtiers: 'Despite of my wishing to do good to this class of worshippers of God, this rogue bears them enmity and thwarts my wish but truth is on his side.'

If a devotee has taken dirhems and dinars
Find another who is more a devotee than he.

'The Sitting Young Man', unknown artist, seventeenth century, Indo Iranian Album, Golestan Palace.

Story 22

A dervish arrived in a place, the owner of which was of a noble disposition, and had surrounded himself with a company of distinguished and eloquent men, each of whom uttered something elegant or jocular, according to the fashion of wits. The dervish who had travelled through the desert and was fatigued had eaten nothing. One of the company asked him by way of encouragement likewise to say something. The dervish replied: 'I do not possess distinction and eloquence like you and have read nothing so you must be satisfied with one distich of mine.' The company having agreed with pleasure he recited:

'I am hungry and opposite to a table of food·
Like a bachelor at the door of a bath of females.'

The company, having thus been apprised of his famished condition, produced a table with bread but as he began to eat greedily the host said: 'Friend, at any rate stop a while till my servants roast some minced meat'; whereon the dervish lifted his head and recited:

'Do not order pounded meat for my table.
To a pounded man simple bread is pounded meat.'

Story 23

A murid said to his pir: 'What am I to do? I am troubled by the people, many of whom pay me visits. By their coming and going they encroach upon my precious time.' He replied: 'Lend something to every one of them who is poor and ask something from every one who is rich and they will come round thee no more.'

If a mendicant were the leader of the army of Islam,
The infidels would for fear of his importunity run as far as China.

Story 24

The son of a faqih said to his father: 'These heart-ravishing words of moralists make no impression upon me because I do not see that their actions are in conformity with their speeches.'

They teach people to abandon the world
But themselves accumulate silver and corn.
A scholar who only preaches and nothing more
Will not impress anyone when he speaks.
He is a scholar who commits no evil,
Not he who speaks to men but acts not himself.

Will you enjoin virtue to mankind and forget your own souls?

A scholar who follows his lusts and panders to his body
Is himself lost although he may show the way.

The father replied: 'My son, it is not proper merely on account of this vain fancy to turn away the face from the instruction of advisers, to travel on the road of vanity, to accuse the ullemma[26] of aberration, and whilst searching for an immaculate scholar, to remain excluded from the benefits of knowledge … The preaching assembly is like the shop of a dealer in linen because if thou bringest no money thou canst obtain no wares and if thou bringest no inclination to the assembly thou wilt not get any felicity.'

Listen with thy soul's ear to a scholar's speech
Although his actions may not be like his doctrines.
In vain does the gainsayer ask:
'How can a sleeper awaken a sleeper?
A man must receive into his ears
The advice although it be written on a wall.'

[26] Scholars.

•

A pious man came to the door of a college from a monastery.
He broke the covenant of the company of those of the Tariq.
I asked him what the difference between a scholar and a monk amounts to?
He replied: 'The former saves his blanket from the waves
Whilst the latter strives to save the drowning man.'

Page from Habib al-Siar *(vol. 2), unknown artist, Golestan Palace.*

Story 25

A man was sleeping dead-drunk on the highway and the bridle of spontaneity had slipped from his hands. A hermit passed near him and considered the disgraceful condition he was in. The youth raised his head and recited:

'When they passed near something contemptible, they passed it kindly.'

When thou beholdest a sinner be concealing and meek.

•

Turn not thy face from a sinner, O anchorite.
Look upon him with benignity.
If I am ignoble in my actions
Pass me by like a noble fellow.

Story 26

A company of vagabonds met a dervish, spoke insulting words to him, struck him and otherwise molested him; whereon he complained to his superior and explained the case. The pir replied: 'My son, the patched frock of dervishes is the garment of resignation and who, wearing it, cannot bear injuries is a pretender not entitled to the frock.'

A large river will not become turbid from stones.
The Arif who feels aggrieved is shallow water yet.

•

If he injures thee, bear it
Because pardon will purify thee from sin.
O brother, as the end is dust,
Be dust before thou art turned into dust.

Story 27

A pious man saw an acrobat in great dudgeon, full of wrath and foaming at the mouth. He asked: 'What is the matter with this fellow?' A bystander said: 'Someone has insulted him.' He remarked: 'This base wretch is able to lift a thousand mann of stones and has not the power to bear one word.'

Abandon thy claim to strength and manliness.
Thou art weak-minded and base, whether thou be a man or woman.
If thou art able, make a sweet mouth.
It is not manliness to strike the fist on a mouth.

•

Although able to tear up an elephant's front
He is not a man who possessed no humanity.
A man's nature is of earth.
If he is not humble he is not a man.

Story 28

I asked a good man concerning the qualities of the brethren of purity. He replied: 'The least of them is that they prefer to please their friends rather than themselves; and philosophers have said that:

A BROTHER WHO IS FETTERED BY AFFAIRS RELATING TO HIMSELF
IS NEITHER A BROTHER NOR A RELATIVE.'

If thy fellow traveller hastens, he is not thy fellow.
Tie not thy heart to one whose heart is not tied to thine.

Story 29

A kind old man in Baghdad
Gave his daughter to a cobbler.
The cruel little man so bit her
That blood flowed from the daughter's lips.
Next morning the father saw her thus
And going to the bridegroom asked him:
'O mean wretch, what teeth are these?
Chewest thou thus her lips? They are not leather.
I do not say these words in jest,
Leave joking off and enjoy her seriously.
If ill humour becomes fixed in a nature
It will not leave it till the time of death.'

Story 30

A sage having been asked whether liberality or bravery is better replied:

'HE WHO POSSESSES LIBERALITY NEEDS NO BRAVERY.'

Hatim Tai has passed away but for ever
His high name will remain celebrated for beneficence.
Set aside the zekat from thy property because the exuberant vines
When pruned by the vintner will yield more grapes.

It is written on the tomb of Behram Gur:
'A liberal hand is better than a strong arm.'

'Excursion in Nature', unknown artist, Sa'di's Bustan, *sixteenth century, Golestan Palace.*

CHAPTER 3

در فضیلت قناعت

ON THE EXCELLENCE OF CONTENTMENT

Story 1

A Maghrabi supplicant said in Aleppo in the row of linen-drapers: 'Lords of wealth, if you were just and we contented, the trade of begging would vanish from the world.'

O contentment, make me rich
For besides thee no other wealth exists.
Loqman selected the corner of patience.
Who has no patience has no wisdom.

Story 2

Two sons of amirs were in Egypt, the one acquiring science, the other accumulating wealth, till the former became the ullemma of the period and the other the prince of Egypt; whereon the rich man looked with contempt upon the faqih and said: 'I have reached the sultanate whilst thou hast remained in poverty as before.' He replied: 'O brother, I am bound to be grateful to the most high Creator for having obtained the inheritance of prophets whilst thou hast attained the inheritance of Pharaoh and of Haman, namely the kingdom of Egypt.'

I am that ant which is trodden under foot
Not that wasp, the pain of whose sting causes lament.
How shall I give due thanks for the blessing
That I do not possess the strength of injuring mankind?

Story 3

I heard that a dervish, burning in the fire of poverty and sewing patch upon patch, said to comfort his mind:

'We are contented with dry bread and a patched robe
For it is easier to bear the load of one's own trouble than that of thanks to others.'

Someone said to him: 'Why sittest thou? A certain man in this town possesses a benevolent nature, is liberal to all, has girded his loins to serve the pious and is ready to comfort every heart. If he becomes aware of thy case, he will consider it an obligation to comfort the mind of a worthy person.' He replied: 'Hush!

It is better to die of inanition than to plead for one's necessities before any man.'

It is better to patch clothes and sit in the corner of patience
Than to write petitions for robes to gentlemen.
Verily it is equal to the punishment of hell
To go to paradise as a flunkey to one's neighbour.

Story 4

Two Khorasani dervishes travelled together. One of them, being weak, broke his fast every second night whilst the other who was strong consumed every day three meals. It happened that they were captured at the gate of a town on suspicion of being spies; whereon each of them was confined in a closet and the aperture of it walled up with mud bricks. After two weeks it became known that they were guiltless. Accordingly the doors were opened and the strong man was found to be dead whilst the weak fellow had remained alive. The people were astonished but a sage averred that the contrary would have been astonishing because one of them having been voracious possessed no strength to suffer hunger and perished whilst the other who was abstemious merely persevered in his habit and remained safe.

When eating little has become the nature of a man
He takes it easy when a calamity befalls him
But when the body becomes strong in affluence
He will die when a hardship overtakes him.

Story 5

One of the philosophers forbade his son to eat much because repletion keeps people ailing. The boy replied: 'O father, it is hunger that kills. Hast thou not heard of the maxim of the ingenious that it is better to die satiated than to bear hunger?' He rejoined:

'BE MODERATE. EAT AND DRINK BUT NOT TO EXCESS.'

Eat not so much that it comes up to thy mouth
Nor so little that from weakness thy soul comes up.

•

Although maintenance of life depends upon food
Victuals bring on disease when eaten to excess.
If thou eatest rose-confectionery without appetite it injures thee
But eating dry bread after a long fast is like rose-preserve.

Story 6

A sick man having been asked what his heart desired replied: 'That it may not desire anything.'

When the bowels are full and the belly pains
There is no use in all other things being right.

Story 7

A grain dealer to whom Sufis were owing some money asked them for it every day in the town of Waset and used harsh language towards them. The companions had become weary of his reproaches but had no other remedy than to bear them; and one of them who was a pious man remarked:

'It is more easy to pacify a hungry stomach with promises of food than a grain dealer with promises of money.'

It is preferable to be without the bounty of a gentleman
Than to bear the insults of the gate-keepers.
It is better to die wishing for meat
Than to endure the expostulations of butchers.

Story 8

A brave warrior who had received a dreadful wound in the Tatar war was informed that a certain merchant possessed a medicine which he would probably not refuse to give if asked for; but it is related that the said merchant was also well known for his avarice.

If instead of bread he had the sun in his table-cloth
No one could see daylight till the day of resurrection.

The warrior replied: 'If I ask for the medicine he will either give it or refuse it and if he gives it maybe it will profit me, and maybe not. At any rate the inconvenience of asking it from him is a lethal poison.'

Whatever thou obtainest by entreaties from base men
Will profit thy body but injure thy soul.

And philosophers have said: 'If for instance the water of life were to be exchanged for a good reputation, no wise man would purchase it because:

It is preferable to die with honour than to live in disgrace.

To eat coloquinth from the hand of a sweet-tempered man
Is better than confectionery from the hand of an ill-humoured fellow.'

'Excursion in Nature', unknown artist, Sa'di's Bustan, *sixteenth century, Golestan Palace.*

Story 9

Hatim Tai, having been asked whether he had seen in the world anyone of more exalted sentiments than himself, replied: 'Yes, one day I slaughtered forty camels to entertain Arab amirs. I had occasion to go out on some business into a corner of the desert, where I noticed a gatherer of briars, who had accumulated a hillock of thistles, and I asked him why he had not become a guest of Hatim since many people had come round to his banquet but he replied:

"Who eats bread by the work of his own hand
Will not bear to be obliged to Hatim Tai."

Then I saw that his sentiments were more exalted than mine.'

Story 10

Moses, to whom be salutation, beheld a dervish who had on account of his nudity concealed himself in the sand exclaiming: 'O Moses, utter a supplication to God the most high to give me an allowance because I am, on account of my distress, on the point of starvation.' Moses accordingly prayed and departed but returning a few days afterwards he saw that the dervish was a prisoner and surrounded by a crowd of people. On asking for the reason he was informed that the dervish had drunk wine, quarrelled, slain a man and was to be executed in retaliation.

If the humble cat possessed wings
He would rob the world of every sparrow-egg.

•

It may happen that when a weak man obtains power
He arises and twists the hands of the weak.

And if Allah were to bestow abundance upon his servants, they would certainly rebel upon earth.

What has made thee wade into danger, O fool,
Till thou hast perished. Would that the ant had not been able to fly!

•

When a base fellow obtains dignity, silver and gold,
His head necessarily demands to be knocked.
Was not after all this maxim uttered by a sage?
'That ant is the best which possesses no wings.'

The heavenly father has plenty of honey but the son has a hot disease.

He who does not make thee rich
Knows better what is good for thee than thyself.

Story 11

I noticed an Arab of the desert sitting in a company of jewellers at Bosrah and narrating stories to them. He said: 'I had once lost my road in the desert and consumed all my provisions. I considered that I must perish when I suddenly caught sight of a bag full of pearls and I shall never forget the joy and ecstasy I felt on thinking they might be parched grain nor the bitterness and despair when I discovered them to be pearls.'

In a dry desert and among moving sand
It is the same to a thirsty man whether he has pearls or shells in his mouth.
When a man has no provisions and his strength is exhausted
It matters not whether his girdle is adorned with pearls or potsherds.

Seventeenth century, Indo Iranian Album, Golestan Palace.

Story 12

I never lamented about the vicissitudes of time or complained of the turns of fortune except on the occasion when I was barefooted and unable to procure slippers. But when I entered the great mosque of Kufah with a sore heart and beheld a man without feet I offered thanks to the bounty of God, consoled myself for my want of shoes and recited:

'A roast fowl is to the sight of a satiated man
Less valuable than a blade of fresh grass on the table
And to him who has no means nor power
A burnt turnip is a roasted fowl.'

Story 13

A king with some of his courtiers had during a hunting party and in the winter season strayed far from inhabited places but when the night set in he perceived the house of a dehqan and said: 'We shall spend the night there to avoid the injury of the cold.' One of the vazirs, however, objected alleging that it was unworthy of the high dignity of a padshah to take refuge in the house of a dehqan and that it would be best to pitch tents and to light fires on the spot. The dehqan who had become aware of what was taking place prepared some food he had ready in his house, offered it, kissed the ground of service and said: 'The high dignity of the sultan would not have been so much lowered, but the courtiers did not wish the dignity of the dehqan to become high.' The king who was pleased with these words moved for the night into the man's house and bestowed a dress of honour upon him the next morning. When he accompanied the king a few paces at the departure he was heard to say:

'Nothing was lost of the sultan's power and pomp
By accepting the hospitality of a dehqan,
But the corner of the dehqan's cap reached the sun
When a sultan such as thou overshadowed his head.'

Story 14

I met a trader who possessed one hundred and fifty camel loads of merchandise with forty slaves and servants. One evening in the oasis of Kish he took me into his apartment and taking all night no rest kept up an incoherent gabble, saying: 'I have such and such a warehouse in Turkestan, such and such goods in Hindostan; this is the title-deed of such and such an estate and in this affair such and such a man is security.' He said: 'I intend to go to Alexandria because it has a good climate', and correcting himself continued: 'No, because the African sea is boisterous. O Sa'di, I have one journey more to undertake and after performing it I shall during the rest of my life sit in a corner and enjoy contentment.' I asked: 'What journey is that?' He replied: 'I shall carry Persian brimstone to China because I heard that it fetched a high price. I shall also carry Chinese porcelain to Rum and Rumi brocade to India and Indian steel to Aleppo, convey glass-ware of Aleppo to Yemen, striped cloth of Yemen to Pares. After that I shall abandon trading and shall sit down in a shop.' He had talked so much of this nonsense that no more strength remained in him so he said: 'O Sa'di, do thou also tell me something of what thou hast seen and heard.' I recited:

'Thou mayest have heard that in the plain of Ghur
Once a leader fell down from his beast of burden,
Saying: "The narrow eye of a wealthy man
Will be filled either by content or by the earth of the tomb."'

Story 15

A weak fisherman caught a strong fish in his net and not being able to retain it the fish overcame him and pulled the net from his hand.

A boy went to bring water from the torrent.
The torrent came and took the boy away.
The net brought every time a fish.
This time the fish went and carried off the net.

The other fishermen were sorry and blamed him for not being able to retain such a fish which had fallen into his net. He replied: 'O brothers, what can be done? My day was not lucky but the fish had yet one remaining.

A FISHERMAN CANNOT CATCH A FISH IN THE TIGRIS WITHOUT A DAY OF LUCK AND A FISH CANNOT DIE ON DRY GROUND WITHOUT THE DECREE OF FATE.'

Story 16

A man whose hands and feet had been amputated killed a millipede and a pious passer-by exclaimed: 'Praised be Allah! In spite of the thousand feet he possessed he could not escape from a man without hands and feet when his fate had overtaken him.'

When the life-taking foe comes in the rear
Fate ties the legs of a running man.
At the moment when the enemy has slowly arrived
It is useless to draw the Kayanian bow.

Gulistan, *from Fatehpur Sikri, India, 1582, Mohammad Hosein Kashmiri, Cambridge Library.*

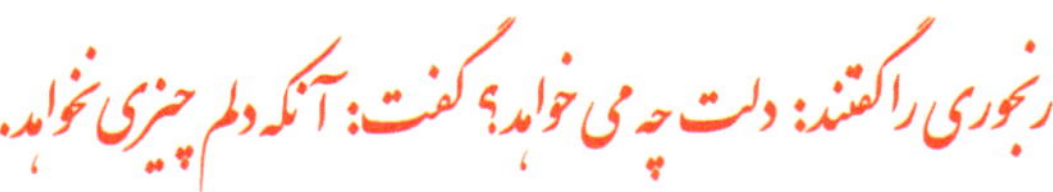

Story 17

It is related that an athlete had been reduced to the greatest distress by adverse fortune. His throat being capacious and his hands unable to fill it, he complained to his father and asked him for permission to travel as he hoped to be able to gain a livelihood by the strength of his arm ...

The father replied: ‘My son, the advantages of travel such as thou hast enumerated them are countless but they regard especially five classes of men:

Firstly, a merchant who possesses in consequence of his wealth and power graceful male and female slaves and quick-handed assistants, alights every day in another town and every night in another place, has recreation every moment and sometimes enjoys the delights of the world.

A rich man is not a stranger in mountain, desert or solitude.
Wherever he goes he pitches a tent and makes a sleeping place;
Whilst he who is destitute of the goods of this world
Must be in his own country a stranger and unknown.

Secondly, a scholar, who is for the pleasantness of his speech, the power of his eloquence and the fund of his instruction, waited upon and honoured wherever he goes.

Thirdly, handsome fellows with whom the souls of pious men are inclined to commingle because it has been said that a little beauty is better than much wealth. An attractive face is also said to be a slave to despondent hearts and the key to locked doors, wherefore the society of such a person is everywhere known to be very acceptable:

I have seen a peacock feather in the leaves of the Quran.
I said: “I see thy position is higher than thy deserts.”

It said: "Hush, whoever is endowed with beauty,
Wherever he places his foot, hands are held out to receive it."

Fourthly, one with a sweet voice, who retains, with a David-like throat, water from flowing and birds from soaring. By means of this talent he holds the hearts of people captive and religious men are delighted to associate with him.

Fifthly, the artisan, who gains a sufficient livelihood by the strength of his arm, so that his reputation is not lost in struggling for bread.

The qualities which I have explained, O my son, are in a journey the occasion of satisfaction to the mind, stimulants to a happy life but he, who possesses none of them, goes with idle fancies into the world and no one will ever hear anything about his name and fame.

He whom the turning world is to afflict
Will be guided by the times against his aim.
A pigeon destined not to see its nest again
Will be carried by fate towards the grain and net.'

The son asked: 'O father, how can I act contrary to the injunctions of the wise, who have said, that:

ALTHOUGH FOOD IS DISTRIBUTED BY PREDESTINATION THE ACQUISITION OF IT DEPENDS UPON EXERTION AND THAT, ALTHOUGH A CALAMITY MAY BE DECREED BY FATE, IT IS INCUMBENT ON MEN TO SHOW THE GATES BY WHICH IT MAY ENTER?

Although daily food may come unawares
It is reasonable to seek it out of doors
And though no one dies without the decree of fate
Thou must not rush into the jaws of a dragon.'

'Crowd Attack the Young Man', unknown artist, Sa'di's Gulistan *(No. 2161), sixteenth century, Golestan Palace.*

After saying this, he asked for the good wishes of his father, took leave of him, departed. He reached the banks of a water, the force of which was such that it knocked stones against each other and its roaring was heard to a farsang's distance.

He beheld a crowd of people, every person sitting with a coin of money at the crossing-place, intent on a passage. The youth's hands of payment being tied, he opened the tongue of laudation and although he supplicated the people greatly, they paid no attention and said:

'No violence can be done to anyone without money
But if thou hast money thou hast no need of force.'

The young man's heart was irritated by the insult of the boatman and longed to take vengeance. The boat had, however, started; so he shouted: 'If thou wilt be satisfied with the robe I am wearing, I shall not grudge giving it to thee.' The boatman was greedy and turned the vessel back.

As soon as the young man's hand could reach the beard and collar of the boatman, he immediately knocked him down and a comrade of the boatman, who came from the vessel to rescue him, experienced the same rough treatment and turned back. The rest of the people then thought proper to pacify the young man and to condone his passage money.

By a sweet tongue, grace, and kindliness,
Thou wilt be able to lead an elephant by a hair.

Then the people fell at his feet, craving pardon for what had passed. They impressed some hypocritical kisses upon his head and his eyes, received him into the boat and started, progressing till they reached a pillar of Yunani workmanship, standing in the water. The boatman said: 'The vessel is in danger. Let one of you, who is the strongest, go to the pillar and take the cable of the boat that we may save the vessel.' The young man, in the pride of bravery which he had in his head, did not think of the offended foe and did not mind the maxim of wise men who have said:

'If thou hast given offence to one man and afterwards done him a hundred kindnesses, do not be confident that he will not avenge himself for that one offence, because although the head of a spear may come out, the memory of an offence will remain in the heart.'

unconcerned for thou wilt be afflicted
If by thy hand a heart has been afflicted.
Throw not a stone at the rampart of a fort
Because possibly a stone may come from the fort.

As soon as he had taken the rope of the boat on his arm, he climbed to the top of the pillar, whereon the boatman snatched it from his grasp and pushed the boat off. The helpless man was amazed and spent two days in misery and distress. On the third, sleep took hold of his collar and threw him into the water. After one night and day he was cast on the bank, with some life still remaining in him. He began to eat leaves of trees and to pull out roots of grass so that when he had gained a little strength, he turned towards the desert and walked till thirst began to torment him. He at last reached a well and saw people drinking water for a pashizi but possessing none he asked for a coin and showed his destitute condition. The people had, however, no mercy with him, whereon he began to insult them but likewise ineffectually. Then he knocked down several men but was at last overpowered, struck and wounded:

A swarm of gnats will overpower an elephant
Despite of all his virility and bravery.
When the little ants combine together
They tear the skin of a furious lion.

As a matter of necessity he lagged in the rear of the caravan, which reached in the evening a locality very dangerous on account of thieves. The people of the caravan trembled in all their limbs but he said: 'Fear nothing because I alone am able to cope with fifty men and the other youths of the caravan will aid me.' These boastful words comforted the heart of the caravan-people, who became glad of his company and considered it incumbent upon themselves to supply him with food and water. The fire of the young man's stomach having blazed into flames and deprived his hands of the bridle of endurance, hunger made him partake of some morsels of food and take a few draughts of water, till the dev of his interior was set at rest and he fell asleep. An experienced old fellow, who was in the caravan, said: 'O ye people, I am more afraid of this guard of yours than of the thieves.

I never sat secure from a serpent
Till I learnt what his custom was.
The wound from a foe's tooth is severe
Who appears to be a friend in the eyes of men.

How do you know whether this man is not one of the band of thieves and has followed us as a spy to inform his comrades on the proper occasion? According to my opinion we ought to depart and let him sleep.' The youths approved of the old man's advice and became suspicious of the athlete, took up their baggage and departed, leaving him asleep. He knew this when the sun shone upon his shoulders and perceived that the caravan had started. He roamed about a great deal without finding the way and thirsty as well as dismayed as he was, he sat down on the ground, with his heart ready to perish, saying:

Who will speak to me after the yellow camels have departed?
A stranger has no companion except a stranger.
He uses harshness towards strangers
Who has not himself been exiled enough.

The poor man was speaking thus whilst the son of a king who happened to be in a hunting party, strayed far from the troops, was standing over his head, listening. He looked at the figure of the athlete, saw that his outward appearance was respectable but his condition miserable. He then asked him whence he had come and how he had fallen into this place. The athlete briefly informed him of what had taken place, whereon the royal prince, moved by pity, presented him with a robe of honour and a large sum of money and sent a confidential man to accompany him till he again

reached his native town. His father was glad to see him and expressed gratitude at his safety. In the evening he narrated to his father what had befallen him with the boat, mentioned the violence of the boatman, the harshness of the rustics near the well and the treachery of the caravan people on the road.

The father replied: 'My son, have not I told thee at thy departure that:

THE BRAVE HANDS OF EMPTY-HANDED PERSONS ARE LIKE THE BROKEN PAW OF A LION?'

The son replied: 'O father:

THOU WILT CERTAINLY NOT OBTAIN A TREASURE EXCEPT BY TROUBLE, WILT NOT OVERCOME THY FOE UNLESS THOU HAZARDEST THY LIFE AND WILT NOT GATHER A HARVEST UNLESS THOU SCATTEREST SEED.

Perceivest thou not how much comfort I gained at the cost of the small amount of trouble I underwent and what a quantity of honey I have brought in return for the sting I have suffered.'

Although not more can be acquired than fate has decreed
Negligence in striving to acquire is not commendable.

•

If a diver fears the crocodile's throat
He will never catch the pearl of great price.

•

What will a fierce lion devour at the bottom of his den?
What food does a fallen hawk obtain?
If thou desirest to catch game at home
Thou must have hands and feet like a spider.

The father said to his son: 'On this occasion heaven has been propitious to thee and good luck helpful so that a royal person has met thee, has been bountiful to thee and has thereby healed thy broken condition. Such coincidences occur seldom and:

The hunter does not catch every time a jackal.
It may happen that some day a tiger devours him.'

Thus it happened that one of the kings of Pares, who possessed a ring with a costly beazle, once went out by way of diversion with some intimate courtiers to the Masalla of Shiraz and ordered his ring to be placed on the dome of Asad, promising to bestow the seal-ring upon any person who could make an arrow pass through it. It happened that every one of the four hundred archers in his service missed the ring, except a little boy who was shooting arrows in sport at random and in every direction from the flat roof of a monastery. The morning breeze caused his arrow to pass through the ring, whereon he obtained not only the ring but also a robe of honour and a present of money. It is related that the boy burnt his bow and arrows and on being asked for the cause replied: 'That the first splendour may be permanent.'

It sometimes happens that an enlightened sage
Is not successful in his plans.
Sometimes it happens that an ignorant child
By mistake hits the target with his arrow.

Story 18

I heard that a dervish, sitting in a cave, had closed the doors upon the face of the world, so that no regard for kings and rich persons remained in the eyes of his desire.

Who opens to himself a door for begging
Will till he dies remain a needy fellow.
Abandon greediness and be a king
Because a neck without desire is high.

One of the kings of that region sent him the information that, trusting in the good manners of the respected dervish, he hoped he would partake of bread and salt with him. The sheikh agreed because it is according to the sonna to accept an invitation. The next day the king paid him a visit, the a'bid leapt up, embraced him, caressed him and praised him. After the monarch's departure the sheikh was asked by one of his companions why he had, against his custom, paid so many attentions to the padshah, the like of which he had never seen before. He replied: 'Hast thou not heard that one of the pious said:

"In whose company thou hast been sitting
To do him service thou must necessarily rise."'

•

Possibly an ear may during a lifetime
Not hear the sound of drum, lute or fife.
The eye may be without the sight of a garden.
The brain may be without the rose or nasrin.
If no feather pillow be at hand
Sleep may be had with a stone under the head
And if there be no sweetheart to sleep with
The hand may be placed on one's own bosom,
But this disreputable twisting belly
Cannot bear to exist without anything.

'In the Presence of the Ascetic', unknown artist, Moraqqa'-e Golestan, *seventeenth century, Golestan Palace.*

'The Wise Scholar and the Arrogant Judge', unknown artist, Sa'di's Bustan *(No. 2164), 1562, Golestan Palace.*

CHAPTER 4

ON THE ADVANTAGES OF SILENCE

Story 1

A merchant, having suffered loss of a thousand dinars, enjoined his son not to reveal it to anyone. The boy said: 'It is thy order and I shall not tell it but thou must inform me of the utility of this proceeding and of the propriety of concealment.' He replied: 'For fear the misfortune would be double; namely, the loss of the money and, secondly, the joy of neighbours at our loss.'

Story 2

An intelligent youth possessed an abundant share of accomplishments and discreet behaviour so that he was allowed to sit in assemblies of learned men but he refrained from conversing with them. His father once asked him why he did not likewise speak on subjects he was acquainted with. He replied: 'I fear I may be asked what I do not know and be put to shame.'

Hast thou heard how a Sufi drove
A few nails under his sandals
And an officer taking him by the sleeve
Said to him: 'Come and shoe my horse.'

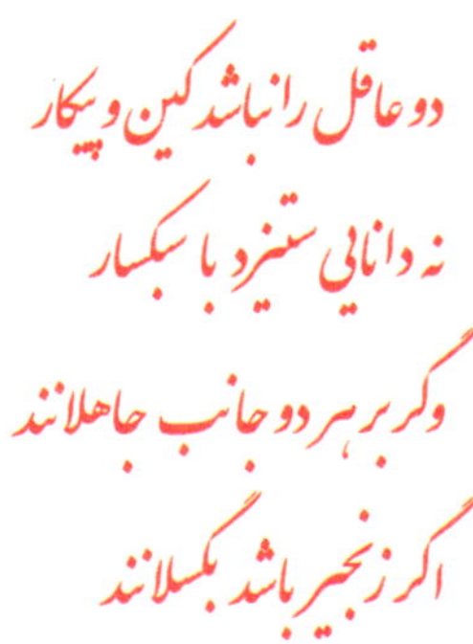

Story 3

Galenus[27] saw a fool hanging on with his hands to the collar of a learned man and insulting him, whereon he said: 'If he were learned he would not have come to this pass with an ignorant man.'

Two wise men do not contend and quarrel
Nor does a scholar fight with a contemptible fellow.
If an ignorant man in his rudeness speaks harshly
An intelligent man tenderly reconciles his heart.
Two pious men keep a hair between them untorn
And so does a mild with a headstrong man.
If however both sides are fools
If there be a chain they will snap it.
An ill-humoured man insulted someone.
He bore it and replied: 'O man of happy issue,
I am worse than thou canst say that I am
Because I know thou art not aware of my faults as I am.'

Story 4

Subhan Vail[28] is considered to have had no equal in rhetorics because he had addressed an assembly during a year and had not repeated the same word but, when the same meaning happened to occur, he expressed it in another manner and this is one of the accomplishments of courtiers and princes.

A word if heart-binding and sweet
Is worthy of belief and of approbation.

[27] Galen.
[28] The great and ancient Arab writer and orator.

When thou hast once said it do not utter it again
Because sweets, once partaken of, suffice.

Story 5

I heard a philosopher say that no one has ever made a confession of his own folly except he who begins speaking, whilst another has not yet finished his talk.

Words have a head, O shrewd man, and a tail.
Do not insert thy words between words of others.
The possessor of deliberation, intelligence and shrewdness
Does not say a word till he sees silence.

Story 6

An astrologer, having entered his own house, saw a stranger and, getting angry, began to insult him, whereon both fell upon each other and fought so that turmoil and confusion ensued. A pious man exclaimed:

'How knowest thou what is in the zenith of the sky
If thou art not aware who is in thy house?'

Story 7

A fellow with a disagreeable voice happened to be reading the Quran, when a pious man passed near, and asked him what his monthly salary was. He replied: 'Nothing.' He further inquired: 'Then why takest thou this trouble?' He replied: 'I am reading for God's sake.' He replied: 'For God's sake do not read.'

If thou readest the Quran thus
Thou wilt deprive the religion of splendour.

'Two Youngsters in the Garden', Shah Qassem, 1592, Reza Abbasi Museum.

CHAPTER 5

در عشق و جوانی

ON LOVE AND YOUTH

Story 1

It is said that a gentleman possessed a slave of exquisite beauty, whom he regarded with love and affection. He nevertheless said to a friend: 'Would that this slave of mine, with all the beauty and good qualities he possesses, had not a long and uncivil tongue!' He replied: 'Brother, do not expect service, after professing friendship; because when relations between lover and beloved come in, the relations between master and servant are superseded':

When a master with a fairy-faced slave
Begins to play and to laugh
What wonder if the latter coquets like the master
And the gentleman bears it like a slave?

Story 2

A schoolboy was so perfectly beautiful and sweet-voiced that the teacher, in accordance with human nature, conceived such an affection towards him that he often recited the following verses:

I am not so little occupied with thee, O heavenly face,
That remembrance of myself occurs to my mind.
From thy sight I am unable to withdraw my eyes
Although when I am opposite I may see that an arrow comes.

Once the boy said to him: 'As thou strivest to direct my studies, direct also my behaviour. If thou perceivest anything reprovable in my conduct, although it may seem approvable to me, inform me thereof that I may endeavour to change it.' He replied: 'O boy, make that request to someone else because the eyes with which I look upon thee behold nothing but virtues.'

The ill-wishing eye, be it torn out
Sees only defects in his virtue.
But if thou possessest one virtue and seventy faults
A friend sees nothing except that virtue.

Story 3

I remember how in former times I and another friend kept company with each other like two almond kernels in one skin. Suddenly a separation took place but after a time, when my companion returned, he commenced to blame me for not having sent him a messenger during it. I replied: 'I thought it would be a pity that the eyes of a messenger should be brightened by thy beauty and I deprived thereof.'

Tell my old friend not to give me advice with the tongue
Because even a sword will not compel me to repent.
I am jealous that anyone should see thee to satiety.
Again I say that no one will be satiated.

Story 4

One of the scholars had been asked that, supposing one sits with a moon-faced beauty in a private apartment, the doors being closed, companions asleep, passion inflamed, and lust raging, as the Arab says, the date is ripe and its guardian not forbidding, whether he thought the power of abstinence would cause the man to remain in safety. He replied:

‘If he remains in safety from the moon-faced one, he will not remain safe from evil speakers.’

If a man escapes from his own bad lust
He will not escape from the bad suspicions of accusers.
It is proper to sit down to one’s own work
But it is impossible to bind the tongues of men.

Story 5

A parrot, having been imprisoned in a cage with a crow, was vexed by the sight and said: ‘What a loathsome aspect is this! What an odious figure! What cursed object with rude habits! O crow of separation, would that the distance of the east from the west were between us.’

Whoever beholds thee when he rises in the morning
The morn of a day of safety becomes evening to him.
An ill-omened one like thyself is fit to keep thee company
But where in the world is one like thee?

More strange still, the crow was similarly distressed by the proximity of the parrot and, having become disgusted, was shouting ‘La haul’, and lamenting the vicissitudes of time. He rubbed the claws of sorrow against each other and said: ‘What ill-luck is this? What base destiny and chameleonlike times? It was befitting my dignity to strut about on a garden-wall in the society of another crow.

It is sufficient imprisonment for a devotee
To be in the same stable with profligates.

What sin have I committed that I have already in this life, as a punishment for it, fallen into the bonds of this calamity in company with such a conceited, uncongenial and heedless fool?’

No one will approach the foot of the wall
Upon which they paint thy portrait.
If thy place were in paradise
Others would select hell.

I have added this parable to let thee know that:

NO MATTER HOW MUCH A LEARNED MAN MAY HATE AN IGNORANT MAN THE LATTER HATES HIM EQUALLY.

A hermit was among profligates
When one of them, a Balkhi beauty, said:
'If thou art tired of us sit not sour
For thou art thyself bitter in our midst.'

•

An assembly joined together like roses and tulips!
Thou art withered wood, growing in its midst,
Like a contrary wind and unpleasant frost,
Like snow inert, like ice bound fast.

Story 6

The beautiful wife of a man died but her mother, a decrepit old hag, remained in the house on account of the dowry. The man saw no means of escaping from contact with her until a company of friends paid him a visit of condolence and one of them asked him how he bore the loss of his beloved. He replied: 'It is not as painful not to see my wife as to see the mother of my wife.'

The rose has been destroyed and the thorn remained.
The treasure has been taken and the serpent left.
It is better that one's eye be fixed on a spear-head
Than that it should behold the face of an enemy.
It is incumbent to sever connection with a thousand friends
Rather than to behold a single foe.

'Salaman Shows Off in the Game of Golf', unknown artist, Salaman va Absal, *1592, Golestan Palace.*

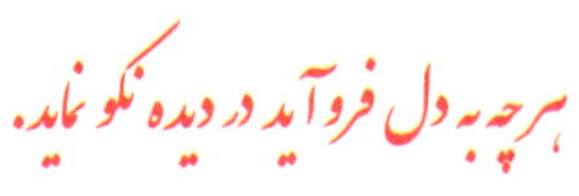

Story 7

A man in patched garments accompanied us in a caravan to the Hejaz and one of the Arab amirs presented him with a hundred dinars to spend upon his family but robbers of the Kufatcha tribe suddenly fell upon the caravan and robbed it clean of everything. The merchants began to wail and to cry, uttering vain shouts and lamentations.

Whether thou implorest or complainest
The robber will not return the gold again.

The dervish alone had not lost his equanimity and showed no change. I asked: 'Perhaps they have not taken thy money?' He replied: 'Yes, they have but I was not so much accustomed to that money that separation therefrom could grieve my heart':

The heart must not be tied to any thing or person
Because to take off the heart is a difficult affair.

I replied: 'That resembles my case: when I was young, my intimacy with a young man and my friendship for him were such that his beauty was the Qiblah of my eye and the chief joy of my life union with him':

Perhaps an angel in heaven but no mortal
Can be on earth equal in beauty of form to him.
I swear by the amity, after which companionship is illicit,
No human sperm will ever become a man like him.

All of a sudden the foot of his life sank into the mire of non-existence. The smoke of separation arose from his family. I kept him company on his grave for many days and one of my compositions on his loss is as follows:

Would that on the day when the thorn of fate entered thy foot
The hand of heaven had struck a sword on my head;

So that this day my eye could not see the world without thee.
Here I am on thy grave, would that it were over my head.

•

He who could take neither rest nor sleep
Before he had first scattered roses and narcissi.
The turns of heaven have strewn the roses of his face.
Thorns and brambles are growing on his tomb.

After separation from him I resolved and firmly determined to fold up the carpet of pleasure during the rest of my life and to retire from mixing in society:

The profit of the sea would be good if there were no fear of waves.
The company of the rose would be sweet if there were no pain from thorns.
Last night I strutted about like a peacock in the garden of union
But today, through separation from my friend, I twist my head like a snake.

Story 8

A king of the Arabs, having been informed of the relations subsisting between Laila and Majnun, with an account of the latter's insanity, to the effect that he had in spite of his great accomplishments and eloquence, chosen to roam about in the desert and to let go the reins of self-control from his hands; he ordered him to be brought to his presence, and this having been done, he began to reprove him and to ask him what defect he had discovered in the nobility of the human soul that he adopted the habits of beasts and abandoned the society of mankind. Majnun replied:

'Many friends have blamed me for loving her.
Will they not see her one day and understand my excuse?'

•

Would that those who are reproving me
Could see thy face, O ravisher of hearts,
That instead of a lemon in thy presence
They might heedlessly cut their hands.

That the truth may bear witness to the assertion: This is he for whose sake ye blamed me.

The king wished to see the beauty of Laila in order to ascertain the cause of so much distress. Accordingly he ordered her to be searched for.

The encampments of various Arab families having been visited, she was found, conveyed to the king and led into the courtyard of the palace. The king looked at her outward form for some time and she appeared despicable in his sight because the meanest handmaids of his harem excelled her in beauty and attractions. Majnun, who shrewdly understood the thoughts of the king, said: 'It would have been necessary to look from the window of Majnun's eye at the beauty of Laila when the mystery of her aspect would have been revealed to thee.'

If the record of the glade which entered my ears
Had been heard by the leaves of the glade they would have lamented with me.
O company of friends, say to him who is unconcerned
'Would that thou knewest what is in a pining heart.'

*

Who are healthy have no pain from wounds.
I shall tell my grief to no one but a sympathizer.
It is useless to speak of bees to one
Who never in his life felt their sting.
As long as thy state is not like mine
My state will be but an idle tale to thee.

Story 9

A virtuous and beauteous youth
Was pledged to a chaste maiden.
I read that in the great sea
They fell into a vortex together.
When a sailor came to take his hand,

Lest he might die in that condition,
He said in anguish from the waves:
'Leave me. Take the hand of my love.'
Whilst saying this, he despaired of life.
In his agony he was heard to exclaim:
'Learn not the tale of love from the wretch
Who forgets his beloved in distress.'
Thus the lives of the lovers terminated.
Learn from what has occurred that thou mayest know
Because Sa'di is of the ways and means of love affairs
Well aware in the Arabian city of Baghdad.
Tie thy heart to the heart-charmer thou possessest
And shut thy eye to all the rest of the world.
If Majnun and Laila were to come to life again
They might indite a tale of love on this occurrence.

Seventeenth century, Indo Iranian Album, Golestan Palace.

'Patience in the Hope of Cure', unknown artist, Sa'di's Bustan *(No. 2164), 1562, Golestan Palace.*

CHAPTER 6

در ضعف و پیری
ON WEAKNESS AND OLD AGE

Story 1

I was holding a disputation with a company of learned men in the cathedral mosque of Damascus when a youth stepped among us, asking whether anyone knew Persian, whereon most of them pointed to me. I asked him what the matter was and he said that an old man, aged one hundred and fifty years, was in the agony of death but saying something in Persian which nobody could understand and that if I were kindly to go and see him I might obtain the information whether he was perhaps desirous of making his last will. When I approached his pillow, he said:

'A while ago I said I shall take some rest
But alas, the way of my breath is choked.
Alas, that from the variegated banquet of life
We were eating a while and told it is enough.'

I interpreted these words in the Arabic language to the Damascenes and they were astonished that despite of his long life he regretted the termination of it so much. I asked him how he felt and he replied: 'What shall I say?'

Hast thou not seen what misery he feels,
The teeth of whose mouth are being extracted?
Consider what his state will be at the hour
When life, so precious to him, abandons his body.

I told him not to worry his imagination with the idea of death and not to allow a hallucination to obtain dominion over his nature because Ionian philosophers have said that although the constitution may be good no

reliance is to be placed on its permanence and although a malady may be perilous it does not imply a full indication of death. I asked: 'If thou art willing, I shall call a physician to treat thee?' He lifted his eyes and said, smiling:

'The skilled doctor strikes his hands together
On beholding a rival prostrate like a potsherd.
A gentleman is engaged in adorning his hall with paintings
Whilst the very foundation of the house is ruined.
An aged man was lamenting in his last agony
Whilst his old spouse was rubbing him with sandal.
When the equilibrium of the constitution is destroyed
Neither incantations nor medicines are of any avail.'

Story 2

It is related that an old man, having married a girl, was sitting with her privately in an apartment adorned with roses, fixing his eyes and heart upon her. He did not sleep during long nights but spent them in telling her jokes and witty stories, hoping to gain her affection and to conquer her shyness. One night, however, he informed her that luck had been friendly to her and the eye of fortune awake because she had become the companion of an old man who is ripe, educated, experienced in the world, of a quiet disposition, who had felt cold and warm, had tried good and bad, who knows the duties of companionship, is ready to fulfil the conditions of love, is benevolent, kind, good-natured and sweet-tongued.

As far as I am able I shall hold thy heart
And if injured I shall not injure in return.
Though sugar may be thy food as of a parrot
I shall sacrifice sweet life to thy support.

Thou hast not fallen into the hands of a giddy youth, fun of whims, headstrong, fickle minded, running about every moment in search of another pleasure and entertaining another opinion, sleeping every night in another place and taking every day another friend. Young men are joyous and of handsome countenance but inconstant in fidelity to anyone.

Expect not faithfulness from nightingales
Who sing every moment to another rose.

Contrary to aged men who spend their lives according to wisdom and propriety; not according to the impulses of folly and youth.

Find one better than thyself and consider it fortunate
Because with one like thyself thou wilt be disappointed.

The old man said: 'I continued in this strain, thinking that I had captivated her heart and that it had become my prey.' She drew, however, a deep sigh from her grief-filled heart and said: 'All the words thou hast uttered, weighed in the scales of my understanding, are not equivalent to the maxim I once heard enounced in my midwife:

"An arrow in the side of a young woman is better than an old man."'

When she perceived in the hands of her husband
Something pendant like the nether lip of a fasting man,
She said: 'This fellow has a corpse with him
But incantations are for sleepers not for corpses.'

•

A woman who arises without satisfaction from a man
Will raise many a quarrel and contention.
An old man who is unable to rise from his place,
Except by the aid of a stick, how can his own stick rise?

In short, there being no possibility of harmony, a separation at last took place. When the time of the lady's uddat had terminated, she was given in marriage to a young man who was violent, ill-humoured and empty-handed. She suffered much from his bad temper and tyrannical

behaviour, and experienced the miseries of penury. She nevertheless said: 'Praise be to Allah for having been delivered from that wretched torment, and attained this permanent blessing.'

Despite of all this violence and hasty nature
I shall try to please thee because thou art beauteous.
To be with thee in hell burning is for me
Better than to be with the other in paradise.
The smell of an onion from the mouth of a pretty face
Is indeed better than a rose from an ugly hand.

'In the Presence of the Ascetic', Aqa Reza, Moraqqa'-e Golshan, *1620, Golestan Palace.*

Story 3

I was in Diarbakr, the guest of an old man, who possessed abundant wealth and a beautiful son. One night he narrated to me that he had all his life no other son but this boy, telling me that in the locality people resorted to a certain tree in a valley to offer petitions and that he had during many nights prayed at the foot of the said tree, till the Almighty granted him this son. I overheard the boy whispering to his companion: 'How good it would be if I knew where that tree is that I might pray for my father to die.' Moral: The gentleman is delighted that his son is intelligent and the boy complains that his father is a dotard.

Years elapse without thy visiting
The tomb of thy father.
What good hast thou done to him
To expect the same from thy son?

Story 4

One day, in the pride of youth, I had travelled hard and arrived perfectly exhausted in the evening at the foot of an acclivity. A weak old man, who had likewise been following the caravan, came and asked me why I was sleeping, this not being the place for it. I replied: 'How am I to travel, having lost the use of my feet?' He said: 'Hast thou not heard that:

It is better to walk gently and to halt now and then than to run and to become exhausted?'

O thou who desirest to reach the station
Take my advice and learn patience.
An Arab horse gallops twice in a race.
A camel ambles gently night and day.

Story 5

In the folly of youth I one day shouted at my mother who then sat down with a grieved heart in a corner and said, weeping:

'HAST THOU FORGOTTEN THY INFANCY THAT THOU ART HARSH TOWARDS ME?'

How sweetly said the old woman to her son
When she saw him overthrow a tiger, and elephant-bodied:
'If thou hadst remembered the time of thy infancy
How helpless thou wast in my arms
Thou would'st this day not have been harsh
For thou art a lion-like man, and I an old woman.'

Story 6

The son of a wealthy but avaricious old man, having fallen sick, his well-wishers advised him that it would be proper to get the whole Quran recited or else to offer a sacrifice. He meditated a while and then said: 'It is preferable to read the Quran because the flock is at a distance.' A holy man, who had heard this, afterwards remarked: 'He selected the reading of the Quran because it is at the tip of the tongue but the money at the bottom of the heart.'

It is useful to bend the neck in prayers
If they are to be accompanied by almsgiving.
For one dinar he would remain sticking in mud like an ass,
But if thou askest for Alhamd[29] *he will recite it a hundred times.*

[29] One of the surahs (parts) of the Quran.

Story 7

An old man, having been asked why he did not marry, replied that he could not be happy with an aged woman, and on being told that as he was a man of property, he might take a young one, he said: 'I being an old man and unwilling to associate with an old woman, how could a young one conceive friendship for me who am aged?'

Let not a man of seventy years make love.
Thou art confessedly blind, kiss her and sleep.
The lady wants strength, not gold.
One passage is preferable to her than ten mann of flesh.

Story 8

I have heard that in these days a decrepit aged man
Took the fancy in his old head to get a spouse.
He married a beauteous little girl, Jewel by name,
When he had concealed his casket of jewels from the eyes of men
A spectacle took place as is customary in weddings.
But in the first onslaught the organ of the sheikh fell asleep.
He spanned the bow but hit not the target; it being impossible to sew
A tight coarse robe except with a needle of steel.
He complained to his friends and showed proofs
That his furniture had been utterly destroyed by her impudence.
Such fighting and contention arose between man and wife
That the affair came before the qazi; and Sa'di said:
'After all this reproach and villainy the fault is not the girl's.
Thou whose hand trembles, how canst thou bore a Jewel?'

Majnun over the dead body of Leila, Nezami's Khamseh, 1536 AD.

CHAPTER 7

ON THE EFFECTS OF EDUCATION

Story 1

A vazir who had a stupid son gave him in charge of a scholar to instruct him and if possible make him intelligent. Having been some time under instruction but ineffectually, the learned man sent to his father with the words: 'The boy is not becoming intelligent and has made a fool of me.'

When a nature is originally receptive
Instruction will take effect thereon.
No kind of polishing will improve iron
Whose essence is originally bad.
Wash a dog in the seven oceans,
He will be only dirtier when he gets wet.
If the ass of Jesus be taken to Mekkah
He will on his return still be an ass.

Story 2

A sage, instructing boys, said to them: 'O darlings of your fathers, learn a trade because property and riches of the world are not to be relied upon; also silver and gold are an occasion of danger because either a thief may steal them at once or the owner spend them gradually.' However:

A PROFESSION IS A LIVING FOUNTAIN AND PERMANENT WEALTH; AND ALTHOUGH A PROFESSIONAL MAN MAY LOSE RICHES, IT DOES NOT MATTER BECAUSE A PROFESSION IS ITSELF WEALTH AND WHEREVER HE GOES HE WILL ENJOY RESPECT AND SIT IN HIGH PLACES, WHEREAS HE WHO HAS NO TRADE WILL GLEAN CRUMBS AND SEE HARDSHIPS:

It is difficult to obey after losing dignity
And to bear violence from men after being caressed.

*

Once confusion arose in Damascus.
Everyone left his snug corner.
Learned sons of peasants
Became the vazirs of padshahs.
Imbecile sons of the vazirs
Went as mendicants to peasants.

Story 3

An illustrious scholar, who was the tutor of a royal prince, had the habit of striking him unceremoniously and treating him severely. The boy, who could no longer bear this violence, went to his father to complain and when he had taken off his coat, the father's heart was moved with pity. Accordingly he called for the tutor and said: 'Thou dost not permit thyself to indulge in so much cruelty towards the children of my subjects as thou inflictest upon my son. What is the reason?' He replied:

'IT IS INCUMBENT UPON ALL PERSONS IN GENERAL TO CONVERSE IN A SEDATE MANNER AND TO BEHAVE IN A LAUDABLE WAY BUT MORE ESPECIALLY UPON PADSHAHS BECAUSE WHATEVER THEY SAY OR DO IS COMMENTED ON BY EVERYBODY, THE UTTERANCES OR ACTS OF COMMON PEOPLE BEING OF NO SUCH CONSEQUENCE.

If a hundred unworthy things are committed by a dervish
His companions do not know one in a hundred.
But if a padshah utters only one jest
It is borne from country to country.

It is the duty of a royal prince's tutor to train up the sons of his lord in refinement of morals – and Allah caused them to grow up as a beautiful plant – more diligently than the sons of common people.

He whom thou hast not punished when a child
Will not prosper when he becomes a man.
While a stick is green, thou canst bend it as thou listest.
When it is dry, fire alone can make it straight.'

The king, being pleased with the appropriate discipline of the tutor and with his explanatory reply, bestowed upon him a robe of honour with other gifts and raised him to a higher position.

Story 4

I saw a schoolmaster in the Maghrib country, who was sour-faced, of uncouth speech, ill-humoured, troublesome to the people, of a beggarly nature and without self-restraint, so that the very sight of him disgusted the Muslims and when reading the Quran he distressed the hearts of the people. A number of innocent boys and little maidens suffered from the hand of his tyranny, venturing neither to laugh nor to speak because he would slap the silver-cheeks of some and put the crystal legs of others into the stocks. In short, I heard that when his behaviour had attained some notoriety, he was expelled from the school and another installed as corrector, who happened to be a religious, meek, good and wise man. He spoke only when necessary and found no occasion to deal harshly with anyone so that the children lost the fear they had entertained for their first master and, taking advantage of the angelic manners of the second, they acted like demons towards each other and, trusting in his gentleness, neglected their studies, spending most of their time in play, and breaking on the heads of each other the tablets of their unfinished tasks.

If the schoolmaster happens to be lenient
The children will play leapfrog in the bazar.

Two weeks afterwards I happened to pass near that same mosque where I again saw the first master whom the people had made glad by reconciliation and had reinstalled in his post. I was displeased, exclaimed

'La haul', and asked why they had again made Iblis the teacher of angels. An old man, experienced in the world, who had heard me, smiled and said: 'Hast thou not heard the maxim?

A padshah placed his son in a school,
Putting in his lap a silver tablet
With this inscription in golden letters:
The severity of a teacher is better than the love of a father.'

Story 5

I saw an Arab of the desert who said to his boy: 'O son, on the day of resurrection thou wilt be asked:

WHAT THOU HAST GAINED AND NOT FROM WHOM THOU ART DESCENDED.

That is to say, thou wilt be asked what thy merit is and not who thy father was.'

The covering of the Ka'bah which is kissed
Has not been ennobled by the silkworm.
It was some days in company with a venerable man
Wherefore it became respected like himself.

هر جا که گل است خار است، و با خمر خمار است و بر سر گنج مار است، و آنجا که درّ شاهوار است نهنگ مردم خوار است.

'Majnun in Desert', Abd-ol-Samad, Moraqqa'-e Golshan, *1551, Golestan Palace.*

Story 6

The wife of a dervish had become enceinte and when the time of her confinement was at hand, the dervish who had no child during all his life said: 'If God the most high and glorious presents me with a son, I shall bestow everything I possess as alms upon dervishes, except this patched garment of mine which I am wearing.' It happened that the infant was a son. He rejoiced and gave a banquet to the dervishes, as he had promised. Some years afterwards when I returned from a journey to Syria, I passed near the locality of the dervish and asked about his circumstances but was told that he had been put in prison by the police. Asking for the cause, I was told that his son, having become drunk, quarrelled and having shed the blood of a man, had fled; whereon his father was instead of him loaded with a chain on his neck and heavy fetters on his legs. I replied: 'He had himself asked God the most high and glorious for this calamity.'

If pregnant women, O man of intellect,
Bring forth serpents at the time of birth,
It is better in the opinion of the wise
Than to give birth to a wicked progeny.

Story 7

An Indian who was learning how to throw naphtha was thus reproved by a sage: 'This is not a play for thee whose house is made of reeds.'

Speak not unless thou knowest it is perfectly proper
And ask not what thou knowest will not elicit a good reply.

Story 8

A little man with a pain in his eyes went to a farrier to be treated by him. The farrier applied to his eyes what he used to put in those of quadrupeds so that the man became blind and lodged a complaint with the judge who, however, refrained from punishing the farrier, saying: 'Had this man not been an ass, he would not have gone to a farrier.' The moral of this story is to let thee know that whoever entrusts an inexperienced man with an important business and afterwards repents is by intelligent persons held to suffer from levity of intellect.

A shrewd and enlightened man will not give
Affairs of importance to a base fellow to transact.
A mat-maker although employed in weaving
Is not set to work in a silk-factory.

Story 9

I noticed the son of a rich man, sitting on the grave of his father and quarreling with a dervish-boy, saying: 'The sarcophagus of my father's tomb is of stone and its epitaph is elegant. The pavement is of marble, tesselated with turquois-like bricks. But what resembles thy father's grave? It consists of two contiguous bricks with two handfuls of mud thrown over it.' The dervish-boy listened to all this and then observed: 'By the time thy father is able to shake off those heavy stones which cover him, mine will have reached paradise.'

An ass with a light burden
No doubt walks easily.

•

A dervish who carries only the load of poverty
Will also arrive lightly burdened at the gate of death
Whilst he who lived in happiness, wealth and ease
Will undoubtedly on all these accounts die hard.
At all events, a prisoner who escapes from all his bonds
Is to be considered more happy than an amir taken prisoner.

'Mystic Riding on Puma', unknown artist, Sa'di's Bustan *(No. 2189), sixteenth century, Golestan Palace.*

Story 10

Contention of Sa'di with a Disputant concerning Wealth and Poverty:

I saw a man in the form but not with the character of a dervish, sitting in an assembly, who had begun a quarrel; and, having opened the record of complaints, reviled wealthy men, alleging at last that the hand of power of dervishes to do good was tied and that the foot of the intention of wealthy men to do good was broken.

The liberal have no money.
The wealthy have no liberality.

I, who had been cherished by the wealth of great men, considered these words offensive and said: 'My good friend, the rich are the income of the destitute and the hoarded store of recluses, ...

It is evident that hungry bowels have but little strength, an empty hand can afford no liberality, shackled feet cannot walk, and no good can come from a hungry belly.

He sleeps troubled in the night
Who has no support for the morrow.
The ant collects in summer a subsistence
For spending the winter in ease.

FREEDOM FROM CARE AND DESTITUTION ARE NOT JOINED TOGETHER AND COMFORT IN POVERTY IS AN IMPOSSIBILITY.

He who possesses means is engaged in worship.
Whose means are scattered, his heart is distracted.

*

The thirsty look in their sleep
On the whole world as a spring of water.

Wherever thou beholdest one who has experienced destitution and tasted bitterness, throwing himself wickedly into fearful adventures and not avoiding their consequences, he fears not the punishment of Yazed and does not discriminate between what is licit or illicit.

The dog whose head is touched by a clod of earth
Leaps for joy, imagining it to be a bone.
And when two men take a corpse on their shoulders,
A greedy fellow supposes it to be a table with food.

Mostly empty handed persons pollute the skirt of modesty by transgression, and those who are hungry steal bread.

What a number of modest women have on account of poverty fallen into complete profligacy, throwing away their precious reputation to the wind of dishonour!

With hunger the power of abstinence cannot abide.
Poverty snatches the reins from the hands of piety.'

Whilst I was uttering these words, the dervish lost the bridle of patience from his hands, drew forth the sword of his tongue, caused the steed of eloquence to caper in the plain of reproach and said: 'Thou hast been so profuse in this panegyric of wealthy men and hast talked so much nonsense that they might be supposed to be the antidote to poverty or the key to the storehouse of provisions; whereas they are a handful of proud, arrogant, conceited and abominable fellows intent upon accumulating property and money and so thirsting for dignity and abundance, that they do not speak to poor people except with insolence, and look upon them with contempt.

They consider scholars to be mendicants and insult poor men on account of the wealth which they themselves possess and the glory of dignity which they imagine is inherent in them. They sit in the highest places and believe they are better than anyone else. They never show kindness to anybody and are ignorant of the maxim of sages that:

He who is inferior to others in piety but superior in riches is outwardly powerful but in reality a destitute man.

If a wretch on account of his wealth is proud to a sage
Consider him to be the podex of an ass, though he may be a perfumed ox.'

I said: 'Do not think it allowable to insult them for they are possessors of generosity.' He rejoined: 'Thou art mistaken. They are slaves of money. Of what use is it that they are like bulky clouds and rain not, like the fountain of light, the sun, and shine upon no one?'

I retorted: 'Thou hast not become aware of the parsimony of wealthy men except by reason of mendicancy or else, to him who has laid aside covetousness, a liberal and an avaricious man would appear to be the same. The touchstone knows what gold is and the beggar knows him who is stingy.' He rejoined: 'I am speaking from experience when I say that they station rude and insolent men at their gates to keep off worthy persons, to place violent hands upon men of piety and discretion, saying: "Nobody is here", and verily they have spoken the truth.'

Of him who has no sense, intention, plan or opinion,
The gatekeeper has beautifully said: 'No one is in the house.'

I said this is excusable because they are teased out of their lives by people expecting favours and driven to lamentation by petitions of mendicants; it being according to common sense:

An impossibility to satisfy beggars even if the sand of the desert were to be transmuted into pearls.

The eye of greediness, the wealthy of the world
Can no more fill than dew can replenish a well.

He said: 'No. I take pity on their state.' I replied: 'No. Thou enviest them their wealth.'

We were thus contending with each other ... At last no arguments remained to him and, having been defeated, he commenced to speak nonsense as is the custom of ignorant men who, when they can no more address proofs against their opponent, shake the chain of enmity.

He falling upon me and I on him,
Crowds running after us and laughing,
The finger of astonishment of a world
On the teeth; from what was said and heard by us.

In short we carried our dispute to the qazi and agreed to abide by a just decision of the judge of Muslims, who would investigate the affair and tell the difference between the rich and the poor. When the qazi had seen our state and heard our logic, he plunged his head into his collar and after meditating for a while spoke as follows: 'O thou, who hast lauded the wealthy and hast indulged in violent language towards dervishes, thou art to know that:

WHEREVER A ROSE EXISTS, THERE ALSO THORNS OCCUR; THAT WINE IS FOLLOWED BY INTOXICATION, THAT A TREASURE IS GUARDED BY A SERPENT, AND THAT WHEREVER ROYAL PEARLS ARE FOUND, MEN-DEVOURING SHARKS MUST ALSO BE. THE STING OF DEATH IS THE SEQUEL OF THE DELIGHTS OF LIFE AND A CUNNING DEMON BARS THE ENJOYMENT OF PARADISE.

What will the violence of a foe do if it cannot touch the seeker of the Friend?
Treasure, serpent; rose, thorn; grief and pleasure are all linked together.

*

If every drop of dew were to become a pearl
The bazar would be full of them as of ass-shells.'

After this the qazi turned the face of reproof from me to the dervish and said: 'O thou who hast alleged that the wealthy are engaged in wickedness and intoxicated with pleasure, some certainly are of the kind thou hast described; of defective aspirations, and ungrateful for benefits received. Sometimes they accumulate and put by, eat and give not; if for instance the rain were to fail or a deluge were to distress the world, they, trusting in their own power, would not care for the misery of dervishes, would not fear God and would say:

If another perishes for want of food
I have some; what cares a duck for the deluge?

*

The base when they have saved their own blankets say:
What boots it if all mankind perishes?

There are people of the kind thou hast heard of, and other persons who keep the table of beneficence spread out, the hand of liberality open, seeking a good name and pardon from God. They are the possessors of this world and of the next, ... '

When the qazi had thus far protracted his remarks and had caused the horse of his eloquence to roam beyond the limits of our expectation, we submitted to his judicial decision, condoned to each other what had passed between us, took the path of reconciliation, placed our heads on each other's feet by way of apology, kissed each other's head and face, terminating the discussion with the following two distichs:

Complain not of the turning of the spheres, O dervish,
Because thou wilt be luckless if thou diest in this frame of mind.
O wealthy man, since thy heart and hand are successful
Eat and be liberal for thou hast conquered this world and the next.

'Story of the Sleeping Passengers and the Frenzied Man', *Abd-ol-Samad Shirin Qalam*, Moraqqa'-e Golshan, *sixteenth century, Golestan Palace*.

CHAPTER 8

در آداب صحبت

MAXIMS AND ADMONITIONS

Rule 1

Property is for the comfort of life, not for the accumulation of wealth. A sage, having been asked who is lucky and who is not, replied: 'He is lucky who has eaten and sowed but he is unlucky who has died and not enjoyed.'

Rule 2

Two men took useless trouble and strove without any profit, when one of them accumulated property without enjoying it, and the other learnt without practising what he had learnt.

However much science thou mayest acquire
Thou art ignorant when there is no practice in thee.
Neither deeply learned nor a scholar will be
A quadruped loaded with some books.
What information or knowledge does the silly beast posses
Whether it is carrying a load of wood or of books?

Rule 3

The country is adorned by intelligent and the religion by virtuous men. Padshahs stand more in need of the advice of intelligent men than intelligent men of the proximity of padshahs.

If thou wilt listen to advice, padshah,
There is none better in all books than this:
'Entrust a business to an intelligent man
Although it may not be his occupation.'

Rule 4

Three things cannot subsist without three things: property without trade, science without controversy and a country without politics.

Rule 5

Speak sometimes in a friendly, conciliatory, manly way
Perhaps thou wilt ensnare a heart with the lasso.
Sometimes speak in anger; for a hundred jars of sugar
Will on occasion not have the effect of one dose of colocynth.

Rule 6

To have mercy upon the bad is to injure the good; to pardon tyrants is to do violence to dervishes.

If thou associatest and art friendly with a wretch
He will commit sin with thy wealth and make thee his partner.

Rule 7

The amity of princes and the sweet voice of children are not to be trusted, because the former is changed by fancy and the latter in the course of one night.

Give not thy heart to a sweetheart of a thousand lovers,
And if thou givest it, thou givest that heart for separation.

Rule 8

Confide not to a friend every secret thou possessest. How knowest thou that he will not some time become thy foe? Inflict not every injury thou canst upon an enemy because it is possible that one day he may become thy friend.

Rule 9

Reveal not to any man the secret which thou desirest to remain concealed, although he may be a friend, because that friend will also have friends, and so on.

Silence is preferable than to tell thy mind
To anyone; saying what is to remain unsaid.
O simpleton, stop the source of the spring.
When it becomes full, the brook cannot be stopped.

Rule 10

A weak foe, who professes submission and shows friendship, has no other object than to become a strong enemy. It has been said that as the friendship of friends is unreliable, what trust can be put in the flattery of enemies?

Rule 11

WHO DESPISES AN INSIGNIFICANT ENEMY RESEMBLES HIM WHO IS CARELESS ABOUT FIRE.

Extinguish it today, while it may be quenched,
Because when fire is high, it burns the world.
Allow not the bow to be spanned
By a foe because an arrow may pierce.

Interpretation of a painting by Kamaleddin Behzad, Sahifeh Banou, seventeenth century, Indo Iranian Album, Golestan Palace.

Rule 12
Speak so between two enemies that thou mayest not be put to shame if they become friends.

Between two men contention is like fire,
The ill-starred back-biter being the wood-carrier.
When both of them become friends again
He will among them be unhappy and ashamed.
To kindle fire between two men
Is not wise but is to burn oneself therein.

•

Converse in whispers with thy friends
Lest thy sanguinary foe may hear thee.
Take care of what thou sayest in front of a wall
Because an ear may be behind the wall.

Rule 13
As long as an affair can be arranged with gold, it is not proper to endanger life.

When the hand is foiled in every stratagem
It is licit to put the hand to the sword.

Rule 14
Wrath beyond measure produces estrangement and untimely kindness destroys authority. Be neither so harsh as to disgust the people with thee nor so mild as to embolden them.

Severity and mildness together are best
Like a bleeder who is a surgeon and also applies a salve.
A wise man uses neither severity to excess
Nor mildness; for it lessens his authority.
He neither exalts himself too much
Nor exposes himself at once to contempt.

•

A youth said to his father: 'O wise man,
Give me for instruction one advice like an aged person.'
He said: 'Be kind but not to such a degree
That a sharp-toothed wolf may become audacious.'

Rule 15

An ill-humoured man is captive in the hands of a foe, from the grasp of whose punishment he cannot be delivered wherever he may go.

If from the hand of calamity an ill-natured man escapes into the sky
The evil disposition of his own nature retains him in calamity.

Rule 16

When thou perceivest that discord is in the army of the foe, be thou at ease; but if they are united, be apprehensive of thy own distress.

Go and sit in repose with thy friends
When thou seest war among the enemies;
But if thou perceivest that they all agree
Span thy bow and carry stones upon the rampart.

Rule 17

WHEN ALL THE ARTIFICES OF AN ENEMY HAVE FAILED HE SHAKES THE CHAIN OF FRIENDSHIP, AND THEREON PERFORMS ACTS OF FRIENDSHIP WHICH NO ENEMY IS ABLE TO DO.

Rule 18

Give not information to a padshah of the treachery of anyone, unless thou art sure he will accept it; else thou wilt only be preparing thy own destruction.

Prepare to speak only when
Thy words are likely to have effect.

Rule 19

WHOEVER GIVES ADVICE TO A SELF-WILLED MAN STANDS HIMSELF IN NEED OF ADVICE.

Rule 20

A fool is pleased by flattery like the inflated heel of a corpse that has the appearance of fatness.

Take care not to listen to the voice of a flatterer
Who expects cheaply to derive profit from thee.
If one day thou failest to satisfy his wishes
He enumerates two hundred faults of thine.

Rule 21

Everyone thinks himself perfect in intellect and his child in beauty.

'Advice of the Ascetic', attributed to Kamaleddin Behzad, Moraqqa'-e Golshan, *sixteenth century, Golestan Palace.*

Rule 22

Ten men eat at a table but two dogs will contend for one piece of carrion. A greedy person will stir, be hungry with the whole world, whilst a contented man will be satisfied with one bread. Wise men have said that poverty with content is better than wealth and not abundance.

Narrow intestines may be filled with dry bread
But the wealth of the surface of the world will not fill a greedy eye.

Rule 23

Whoever does no good in the time of ability will see distress in the time of inability.

No one is more unlucky than an oppressor of men
Because in the day of calamity no one is his friend.

Rule 24

WHATEVER TAKES PLACE QUICKLY IS NOT PERMANENT.

A little fowl issues from the egg and seeks food
Whilst man's progeny has no knowledge, sense or discernment.
Nevertheless the former attains nothing when grown up
Whilst the latter surpasses all beings in dignity and excellence.
Glass is everywhere, and therefore of no account,
But a ruby difficult to get, and therefore precious.

Rule 25

AFFAIRS SUCCEED BY PATIENCE AND A HASTY MAN FAILS.

I saw with my eyes in the desert
That a slow man overtook a fast one.
A galloping horse, fleet like the wind, fell back
Whilst the camel-man continued slowly his progress.

نادان را به از خامشی نیست وگر این مصلحت بدانستی نادان نبودی.

Rule 26

Nothing is better for an ignorant man than silence, and if he were to consider it to be suitable, he would not be ignorant.

If thou possessest not the perfection of excellence
It is best to keep thy tongue within thy mouth.
Disgrace is brought on a man by his tongue.
A walnut, having no kernel, will be light.

•

A fool was trying to teach a donkey,
Spending all his time and efforts in the task.
A sage observed: 'O ignorant man, what sayest thou?
Fear blame from the censorious in this vain attempt.
A brute cannot learn speech from thee.
Learn thou silence from a brute.'

•

Who does not reflect what he is to answer
Will mostly speak improperly.
Come. Either arrange thy words like a wise man
Or remain sitting silent like a brute.

Rule 27

Whenever a man disputes with one who is more learned than himself to make people know of his learning, they will know that he is ignorant.

Rule 28

Reveal not the secret faults of men because thou wilt put them to shame and wilt forfeit thy own confidence.

Rule 29

Who acquires science and does not practise it, resembles him who possesses an ox but does not use him to plough or to sow seed.

Rule 30
Not everyone who is handsome in form possesses a good character; the qualities are inside not upon the skin.

It is possible in one day to know from a man's qualities
What degree of science he has reached.
Be however not sure of his mind nor deceived.
A wicked spirit is not detected sometimes for years.

Rule 31
It is preferable to respite captives because the option of killing or not killing remains; but if they be slain without delay, it is possible that some advantage may be lost, the like of which cannot be again obtained.

It is quite easy to deprive a man of life.
When he is slain he cannot be resuscitated again.
It is a condition of wisdom in the archer to be patient
Because when the arrow leaves the bow it returns no more.

Rule 32
When a sage comes in contact with fools, he must not expect to be honoured, and if an ignorant man overcomes a sage in an oratorical contest, it is no wonder, because even a stone breaks a jewel.

What wonder is there that the song
Of a nightingale ceases when imprisoned with a crow.

•

Or that a virtuous man under the tyranny of vagabonds
Feels affliction in his heart and is irate.
Although a base stone may break a golden vase,
The price of the stone is not enhanced nor of the gold lost.

Rule 33
Even after falling into mud a jewel retains its costliness, and dust, though it may rise into the sky, is as contemptible as before. Capacity without education is deplorable and education without capacity is thrown away.

Ashes are of high origin because the nature of fire is superior, but as they have no value of their own, they are similar to earth and the price of sugar arises not from the cane but from its own quality.

Rule 34

MUSK IS KNOWN BY ITS PERFUME AND NOT BY WHAT THE DRUGGIST SAYS. A SCHOLAR IS SILENT LIKE THE PERFUMER'S CASKET BUT DISPLAYS ACCOMPLISHMENTS, WHILST AN IGNORAMUS IS LOUD-VOICED AND INTRINSICALLY EMPTY LIKE A WAR-DRUM.

A learned man among blockheads
(So says the parable of our friends)
Is like a sweetheart among the blind
Or a Quran among unbelievers.

Rule 35

A friend whom people have been cherishing during a lifetime they must not suddenly insult.

It takes a stone many a year to become a ruby.
Beware not to break it in a moment with a stone.

Rule 36

A LIBERAL MAN WHO EATS AND BESTOWS IS BETTER THAN A DEVOTEE WHO FASTS AND HOARDS.

Rule 37

LITTLE BY LITTLE BECOMES MUCH AND DROP BY DROP WILL BE A TORRENT.

That is to say, he who has no power gathers small stones that he may at the proper opportunity annihilate the pride of his foe.

Drop upon drop collected will make a river.
Rivers upon rivers collected will make a sea.
Little and little together will become much.
The granary is but grain upon grain.

Rule 38

A scholar is not meekly to overlook the folly of a common person because thus both parties are injured; the dignity of the former being lessened, and the ignorance of the latter confirmed.

Speak gracefully and kindly to a low fellow,
His pride and obstinacy will augment.

Rule 39

It is better to be an ignorant poor fellow
Then a learned man who is not abstemious;
Because the former loses the way by his blindness
While the latter falls into a well with both eyes open.

From Sa'di's Bustan, *unknown artist, 1553, Golestan Palace.*

Rule 40

Forbear to wish evil to an envious man
Because the ill-starred fellow is an evil to himself.
What needest thou to show enmity to him
Who has such a foe on the nape of his neck?

Rule 41

One being asked what a learned man without practice resembled, replied: 'A bee without honey.'

Say to the rude and unkind bee,
'At least forbear to sting, if thou givest no honey.'

Rule 42

Although a sultan's garment of honour is dear, yet one's own old robe is more dear; and though the food of a great man may be delicious, the broken crumbs of one's own sack are more delicious.

Vinegar by one's own labour and vegetables
Are better than bread received as alms, and veal.

Rule 43

It is contrary to what is proper, and against the common opinion to partake of medicine by guess and to go after a caravan without seeing the road. The Imam Murshid Muhammad Ghazali, upon whom be the mercy of Allah, having been asked in what manner he had attained such a degree of knowledge, replied: 'By not being ashamed to ask about things I did not know.'

The hope of recovery is according to reason,
That he should feel thy pulse who knows thy nature.
Ask what thou knowest not; for the trouble of asking
Will indicate to thee the way to the dignity of knowledge.

Rule 44

Whatever thou perceivest will become known to thee in due course of time. Make no haste in asking for it, else the awe of thy dignity will be lessened.

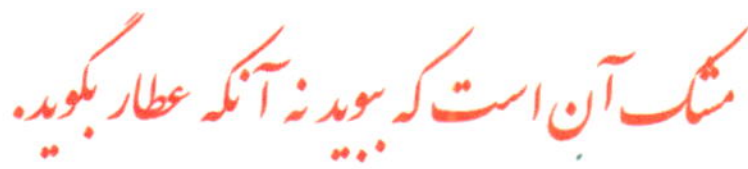

Rule 45
Anyone associating with bad people, although their nature may not infect his own, is supposed to follow their ways to such a degree that if he goes to a tavern to say his prayers, he will be supposed to do so for drinking wine.

Thou hast branded thyself with the mark of ignorance,
When thou hast selected an ignoramus for thy companion.
I asked some scholars for a piece of advice.
They said: 'Connect thyself not with an ignorant man,
For if thou be learned, thou wilt be an ass in course of time
And if unlearned thou wilt become a greater fool.'

Rule 46
The meekness of the camel is known to be such that if a child takes hold of its bridle and goes a hundred farsakhs, it will not refuse to follow, but if a dangerous portion occurs which may occasion death and the child ignorantly desires to approach it, the camel tears the bridle from his hand, refusing any longer to obey because compliance in times of calamity is blamable. It is also said that by complaisance an enemy will not become a friend but that his greed will only be augmented.

To him who is kind to thee, be dust at his feet
But if he opposes thee fill his two eyes with dust.
Speak not kindly or gently to an ill-humoured fellow
Because a soft file cannot clean off inveterate rust.

Rule 47
Who interrupts the conversation of others that they may know his excellence, they will become acquainted only with the degree of his folly.

An intelligent man will not give a reply
Unless he be asked a question.
Because though his words may be based on truth,
His claim to veracity may be deemed impossible.

Rule 48
I had a wound under my robe and a sheikh asked me daily how, but not where it is, and I learned that he refrained because it is not admissible to mention every member; and wise men have also said that:

WHOEVER DOES NOT PONDER HIS QUESTION WILL BE GRIEVED BY THE ANSWER.

Until thou knowest thy words to be perfectly suitable
Thou must not open thy mouth in speech.
If thou speakest truth and remainest in captivity,
It is better than that thy mendacity deliver thee therefrom.

'Hunting Ground', attributed to Kamaleddin Behzad, Moraqqa'-e Golshan, *sixteenth century, Golestan Palace.*

Rule 49

Mendacity resembles a violent blow, the scar of which remains, though the wound may be healed. Seest thou not how the brothers of Joseph became noted for falsehood, and no trust in their veracity remained.

One habitually speaking the truth
Is pardoned when he once makes a slip
But if he becomes noted for lying,
People do not believe him even when speaking truth.

Rule 50

Fortunate men are admonished by the adventures and similes of those who have preceded them, before those who follow them can use the event as a proverb, like thieves who shorten their hands, lest their hands be cut off.

The bird does not go to the grain displayed
When it beholds another fowl in the trap.
Take advice by the misfortunes of others
That others may not take advice from thee.

Rule 51

A mendicant with a good end is better than a padshah with a bad end.

The grief thou sufferest before the joy
Is better than the grief endured after joy.

Rule 52

Gold is obtained from a mine by digging it, but from a miser by digging the soul.

Vile men spend not, but preserve.
They say hope of spending is better than spending.
One day thou seest the wish of the foe fulfilled
The gold remaining and the vile man dead.

Rule 53
Who has no mercy upon inferiors will suffer from the tyranny of superiors.

Not every arm which contains strength
Breaks the hand of the weak for showing bravery.
Injure not the heart of the helpless
For thou wilt succumb to the force of a strong man.

Rule 54
When a wise man encounters obstacles, he leaps away and casts anchor at the proper opportunity, for thus he will be in the former instance safe on shore, and in the latter he will enjoy himself.

Rule 55
The gambler requires three sixes and only three aces turn up.

The pasture is a thousand times more pleasant than the racecourse
But the steed has not the bridle at its option.

Rule 56
A dervish prayed thus: 'O Lord, have mercy upon the wicked, because thou hast already had mercy upon good men by creating them to be good.'

Rule 57
The teeth of all men are blunted by sourness, but those of the qazi by sweetness.

Rule 58
Two men died, bearing away their grief. One had possessed wealth and not enjoyed it, the other knowledge and not practised it.

No one sees an excellent but avaricious man
Without publishing his defect
But if a liberal man has a hundred faults
His generosity covers his imperfections.

CONCLUSION OF THE BOOK

The book of the Gulistan has been completed, and Allah had been invoked for aid! By the grace of the Almighty, may his name be honoured, throughout the work the custom of authors to insert verses from ancient writers by way of loan, has not been followed.

To adorn oneself with one's own rag
Is better than to ask for the loan of a robe.

Most of the utterances of Sa'di being exhilarant and mixed with pleasantry, shortsighted persons have on this account lengthened the tongue of blame, alleging that it is not the part of intelligent men to spend in vain the kernel of their brain, and to eat without profit the smoke of the lamp; it is, however, not concealed from enlightened men, who are able to discern the tendency of words, that pearls of curative admonition are strung upon the thread of explanation, and that the bitter medicine of advice is commingled with the honey of wit, in order that the reader's mind should not be fatigued, and thereby excluded from the benefit of acceptance; and praise be to the Lord of both worlds.

We gave advice in its proper place
Spending a lifetime in the task.
If it should not touch anyone's ear of desire
The messenger told his tale; it is enough.

ACKNOWLEDGEMENTS

Consultant and collaborator on image and photo selection: Fatemeh Samadi.

Sources of the images:

A Manuscript of the Gulistan (Rosegarden) by Sa'di; Sa'di in a Rose garden, Smithsonian's National Museum of Asian Art

– *A Survey of Persian Art From Pre-Historic Times to the Present*, by Arthur Upham Pope and Phyllis Ackerman; Oxford: OUP, 1938

– *Indo Iranian Album*, Iranian Academy of Arts, Tehran, 2022

– *Islamic Bookbindings in The Victoria and Albert*, by Duncan Haldane; World of Islam Festival Trust, in association with Victoria and Albert Museum, 1983

– *Masterpices of Persian Paintings*, Tehran Museum of Contemporary Art, second edition, 2011, Tehran, Iran

– *Selections From the Bustan*, No. 2167 (Manuscript with illustrations), Golestan Palace Library, Tehran

– *The Art and Architecture of Islam* (1250–1800), by Sheila Blair and Jonathan M. Bloom; Yale University Press, 1996

– *The Bustan (Orchard) of Sa'di*, 936–1529 AD, The Metropolitan Museum of Art, New York

– *The Bustan of Sa'di*, No.2164 (manuscript with illustrations), Golestan Palace Library, Tehran

– *The Bustan of Sa'di*, No.2189 (manuscript with illustrations), Golestan Palace Library, Tehran

– *The Bustan of Sa'di*, No.2197 (manuscript with illustrations), Golestan Palace Library, Tehran

– *The Bustan of Sa'di*, K.S. 582, Reza Abbasi Museum (manuscript with illustrations), Tehran

– *The Gulistan of Sa'di*, by Mohammad Hosein Kashmiri; Cambridge Library, Fatehpur Sikri, India, 1582

– *The Gulistan of Sa'di*, No. 2161 (manuscript with illustrations), Golestan Palace Library, Tehran

– *The Complete Works (Kolliyat) of Sa'di*, No. 2174 (manuscript with illustrations), Golestan Palace Library, Tehran

– *The Moraqqa-e Golshan* (Golshan Album), Golestan Palace Library, Tehran

– *The Rebellious Reformer: The Drawings and Paintings of Riza-Yi Abbasi of Isfahan*, by Sheila R. Canby; London: I.B.Tauris, 1996

– *The World of Islam: Faith, People, Culture*, edited by Bernard Lewis; London: Thames and Hudson, 1976